Apocalyptic Fervor

Apocalyptic Fervor

Visions of the End Times

KEN BAZYN

RESOURCE *Publications* · Eugene, Oregon

APOCALYPTIC FERVOR
Visions of the End Times

Copyright © 2022 Ken Bazyn. All rights reserved. Except for brief quotations in critical publications or reviews, no part of this book may be reproduced in any manner without prior written permission from the publisher. Write: Permissions, Wipf and Stock Publishers, 199 W. 8th Ave., Suite 3, Eugene, OR 97401.

Resource Publications
An Imprint of Wipf and Stock Publishers
199 W. 8th Ave., Suite 3
Eugene, OR 97401

www.wipfandstock.com

PAPERBACK ISBN: 978-1-6667-4842-0
HARDCOVER ISBN: 978-1-6667-4843-7
EBOOK ISBN: 978-1-6667-4844-4

11/17/22

New Revised Standard Version, copyright 1989, Division of Christian Education of the National Council of Churches in the United States of America. Used by permission. All rights reserved.

Contents

Acknowledgments | vii
Introduction: Heaven, A Fantasy with Explanatory Digressions | ix

A Day Like No Other | 2
Deceitful Time | 4
All Is Smoke | 6
Time Is . . . . | 9
The Whining Mandolin | 12
The Dance of Death | 14
Delusion | 17
A Night of Peacock Eyes | 19
The Reluctant Left Hand of My God | 23
"There Was Silence . . ." | 26
The Meaning Flowed On | 28
On a June Evening | 30
"Nichts als Mauern" | 32
Orwellian Tremors | 34
Now Is Madness Come of Age | 36
I Shall Go Berserk | 39
Touching Bottom | 42
The Light Which Had Been So Keen and Focused | 45
Night Turbulence | 47
Ludicrous Babylon | 49

An Oblong, Inscrutable Alien | 51
Narcissism | 53
Marital Ecology | 55
Our Heap of Merits | 57
Approach-Avoid God | 60
Disembodied You | 63
The Lingerers at Krakatoa | 65
The House of the Lord | 67
A Redemptorist Monk | 69
My Soul | 72
Penetrating Light | 74
Variations on a Medieval Legend | 76
Morituri te Salutamus | 78
O Night That Doomed Leviathan | 81
The Apocalypse | 84
If I Could But Touch Peace... | 87
The Paschal Candle | 89
A Baaing Lamb | 91
How Shall the Dead Arise? | 93
Revelation 7:9–10 | 95
To What Shall I Compare the Kingdom of Heaven? | 98
Come, Holy Spirit | 100
A Rabelaisian Yuletide | 103
Iacta Alea Esto | 108
Numeral Occult | 110
Soul Vibes | 113
Yurodivy: The Holy Fool | 115
That Amethyst Chariot | 117
When the Soul Quits the Earthly Body | 119
On Eternity's Shore Looking Back | 121
II Corinthians 3 | 123

Listing of Photographs | 125
Works Cited | 129

Acknowledgments

How GOOD IT IS to see Wipf & Stock publishing so many intriguing poetry books from varied viewpoints to reach an audience for both emerging and mature stylists. I would also like to express my admiration for Savanah N. Landerholm's obvious typesetting and layout talents as well as to Rockbrook Camera in Omaha for artfully turning my 35mm color slides into high quality jpegs.

Of course, no book of mine could be complete without mentioning my wife, Barbara, who has critically evaluated each and every line to improve both sound and meaning, while the ever-zealous David Reynolds has occupied himself with questions of style, grammar, and formatting, so the book flows effortlessly.

The following appeared previously:
"Marital Ecology" in *Pierian Spring*
An embryonic version of "Heaven: A Fantasy" in *The Living Church*

Introduction

Heaven, A Fantasy with Explanatory Digressions

post tot naufragia portum
("after so many shipwrecks, the harbor")[1]

ANSELM, AQUINAS, AUGUSTINE. My head aches from all this reading. It's almost 11:30 and I need to sleep. Just one more book before I rest, just one more. (Please bear with me during this flight of fancy, as I make a fictional visit to heaven.)

I felt like I was climbing an endless ladder through the troposphere, through the stratosphere, through the ionosphere, until I entered into the most incredible realm known to man or beast. Think of that upward-extending bronze ladder in the extraordinary vision of the early third-century Christian martyr Perpetua.[2] "Eye hath not seen, nor ear heard, neither have entered into the heart of man," the Apostle Paul told the Corinthians, "the things which God hath prepared for them that love him" (1 Cor. 2:9 KJV). The abode of God is beyond our wildest imaginings. In *Paradiso*, Dante coined the term *trasumanar* (meaning "to go beyond the human"), since earthly concepts could not adequately express

---

1. Mawson, *Dictionary of Foreign Terms*, 278.

2. "The Martyrdom of Saints Perpetua and Felicitas," Kramer, *Maenads, Martyrs, Matrons, Monastics*, 98.

the wonders he beheld.³ Heaven resembles an earthly city, yet it also confers the delights of a garden paradise.

Before me stood an imposing wall, surrounding the city; there were twelve gates, three per side. Each was guarded by an angel and inscribed with one of the names of the twelve tribes of Israel (Rev. 21:12–13). Inside this enclosure was a majestic, crystal river coursing down the city's main boulevard.⁴ On either bank were life-giving trees bearing twelve kinds of fruit: one for each month of the year, as well as leaves for the healing of the nations (Rev. 22:1–2). Recall Latin satirist Lucian's imaginative depiction of the Island of the Blessed, where grape vines yielded twelve vintages a year, while apple, pomegranate, and other fruit trees produced thirteen crops.⁵

And the earth gave forth its abundance freely; no plowing or sowing was required. In the shade of the trees rested a fantastic menagerie—gazelles alongside lions, rabbits beside coyotes, house flies near spiders—as if the predator/prey relationship no longer existed. The scene recalled "The Peaceable Kingdom" by American primitive artist Edward Hicks, arising from millennial visions in the Old Testament such as Isaiah 11:6: "The wolf shall live with the lamb, the leopard shall lie down with the kid, the calf and the lion and the fatling together, and a little child shall lead them."⁶ Was no one afraid in this new-found land? Everywhere serenity reigned. Twelve pearl gates, covered with ivy, lay open and inviting, as though they hadn't been shut for centuries. Standing upright, they resembled giant guest books, since upon them had been scribbled a million times a million signatures.

I cautiously stepped in, expecting to behold some decaying archaeological ruin. Instead, the city itself was pure gold, transparent as glass (Rev. 21:18); I almost needed sunglasses to shield my eyes. One can catch a sense of this incandescent yellow from Gustave Doré's nineteenth-century engravings.⁷ Centuries before, the temple of Solomon and its entire inner sanctuary, too, had been overlaid with gold (1 Kings 6:20–22). Had I somehow entered into El Dorado and the Seven Cities of Gold which had so enthralled the conquistadors' quest? On the wall's foundations were the names of each of Christ's twelve apostles (Rev. 21:14), much like

---

3. Russell, *A History of Heaven*, 165.

4. How different this is from the historical city of David, which was dependent on two nearby springs.

5. "A True Story," Lucian, *Selected Satires*, 38.

6. Richardson, *A Short History of Painting*, 151–53.

7. Hind, *The Faces of God*, 161.

the walls of Uruk in ancient Sumeria had been laid by seven wise men, according to *The Epic of Gilgamesh*.[8] The foundation itself was an iridescent colorama of precious stones of every hue: jasper, sapphire, agate, emerald, onyx, carnelian, chrysolite, beryl, topaz, chrysoprase, jacinth, and amethyst (Rev. 21:19-20)—gleaming like the twelve stones on the high priest's breastplate.[9] Likewise, in Lucian's Island of the Blessed, one entered into a golden metropolis, surrounded by emerald walls having seven gates of cinnamon-wood, its streets and foundations of ivory.[10]

I was gazing at the New Jerusalem depicted in the closing chapters of the Book of Revelation by John of Patmos. It was shaped like a cube, 12,000 stadia (about 1500 miles) to a side (Rev. 21:16). To perceive how enormous this is, consider that the walls which surrounded great urban centers in the ancient world, like Babylon and Alexandria, were a mere nine miles in circumference.[11] The Holy of Holies in Solomon's temple had also been a cube (1 Kings 6:20). At New Jerusalem's center stood a double throne for God and the Lamb—their presence being so radiant there was no need for either the sun or the moon (Rev. 21:22-23). In a midrash on Exodus 27:20, the Holy One of Israel announced: "In this world you needed the light of the Temple, but in the world to come . . . I will bring you the King Messiah, who is compared to a lamp, as it is written, 'There I will make a horn to sprout for David, I have prepared a lamp for my Messiah' (Ps. 132:17). And not only this: I will make light for you, because this is what Isaiah said: 'The Lord will be your [i.e. Jerusalem's] everlasting light, and your God will be your glory' (Isa. 60:19)."[12]

The city serves as a magnet for earth's rulers, who bring in the glory of the nations (Rev. 21:24, 26). "And the ships come from En Gedi to Eglayim, laden with riches and honors for the pious," adds Sefer Eliahu.[13] Its purity will be like "the city of righteousness" in Theravada Buddhism, which, according to the *Questions of King Menander*, had "virtue for its ramparts, fear of sin for its moat, knowledge for its gates, zeal for its turrets, faith for its pillars, concentration for its watchmen, wisdom for its palaces."[14]

---

8. Aune, *Revelation*, 17-22, 1157. Cf. Speiser, "The Epic of Gilgamesh," 40.
9. Beale, *Revelation*, 486.
10. Lucian, *Selected Satires*, 38.
11. Aune, *Revelation* 17-22, 1160.
12. Aune, *Revelation* 17-22, 1170.
13. Patai, *Messiah Texts*, 238.
14. Trenckner, "Milindapanha," 113.

I observed an almost endless choir of angels singing tunes from my childhood, "Come, Ye Faithful, Raise the Strain," "All Creatures of Our God and King," "A Mighty Fortress Is Our God," "Shall We Gather at the River," plus new melodies I gladly would have learned, but curiosity impelled me on. Recall how the heavenly host suddenly burst into song at Christ's own birth (Lk. 2:13–14). These fiery creatures sang in a language I had never heard before, yet somehow could understand. When they moved their lips, it seemed as if their whole bodies were in motion, so earnest was their praise. And unlike orchestras I was attuned to on earth, the choruses didn't succeed one after another, but all were being played simultaneously. I could join in any, or all, at will. I heard an antiphon to God as creator (Rev. 4:11), a psalm to Christ as the lamb that was slain (Rev. 5:9–10), as well as that ever-recurring refrain, "Holy, holy, holy, the Lord God the Almighty" (Rev. 4:8). The angels were joined by righteous martyrs (Rev. 6:9–11, 16:7), 144,000 taken out of the twelve tribes of Israel (Rev. 7:4), as well as "a great multitude that no one could count, from every nation, from all tribes and peoples and languages" (Rev. 7:9). What a paean to cosmic diversity! In *Paradiso*, canto 30, Dante had counted more than 1000 tiers of saints—some who had been born before Christ and some born after—in an amphitheater whose lowest, smallest tier had a circumference greater than the sun.[15]

Harps were being played, palm leaves waved amid a continuous tumult of praise and rejoicing, while incense was burned on an altar before the throne (Rev. 5:8, 7:9, 8:4). "O, walk 'em easy round de heaven," declares an African-American spiritual, "O, shout glory till 'em join dat band!"[16] In Lucian's Elysian Fields, one also finds boys' and girls' choirs, such renowned composers as Arion and Anacreon, as well as choruses of swans, swallows, and nightingales—accompanied by an entire forest being conducted by the wind.[17] In a similar fashion, in the Hindu text *Bhagavata Purana*, when Bali had ousted Indra as ruler of heaven, one heard "the booming of *mrdanga*, the sounds of conch and kettle-drum, the music of *vina* and tambourine, *rshti*, and flute, and cymbals . . . and the singing of the demigods."[18]

---

15. Gallagher, *To Hell and Back with Dante*, 192.
16. Sernett, ed., *Afro-American Religious History*, 119.
17. Lucian, *Selected Satires*, 39.
18. Zaleski and Zaleski, eds., *Book of Heaven*, 219.

Four exotic creatures appeared around the throne having six wings and myriad eyes (Rev. 4:6–8), one each in the likeness of a lion, an ox, a human being, and a flying eagle, much like the figures in Ezekiel's vision (Ezek. 1:4–8). There were twenty-four lesser seats for twenty-four elders clad in white robes and golden crowns. In the foreground stood seven flaming torches, as well as a sea of glass; behind this was a rainbow being interrupted by flashes of lightning and peals of thunder (Rev. 4:3–6). In the fifteenth century, artist Hans Memling created an altarpiece depicting this heavenly throne room—placing it inside a circular rainbow shaped like an eyeball.[19] Beginning in the eleventh century, German and French churches hung enormous chandeliers in their apses, known as Jerusalem crowns. These consisted of golden circles or polygons representing the walls of New Jerusalem and were decorated with images from Revelation chapter 21. The large number of candles (forty-eight, seventy-two, or ninety-six) depicted how God's splendor would illuminate the entire city.[20]

Within the heavenly city, human beings were jetting to-and-fro as if in a science fiction film. Some I recognized—a neighbor who had had his arm blown off during the war, was using his right limb again; a widow who had always seemed on the verge of tears now appeared nearly radiant; a disheveled bum I used to pass on my way to work now stood a new man from head to foot. Just as Isaiah had prophesied, "Then the eyes of the blind shall be opened, and the ears of the deaf unstopped; then the lame shall leap like a deer, and the tongue of the speechless sing for joy," (Isa. 35:5–6). I met those whom Cyprian, Bishop of Carthage, had referred to as "God's friends,"[21] from the famous—Abraham and Sarah, Jeremiah and Ezekiel, Peter and Paul, John Chrysostom and Basil of Caesarea, Francis of Assisi and Thomas Aquinas, Luther and Calvin, Teresa of Avila and Susanna Wesley, Fyodor Dostoyevsky and Shusaku Endo, Frederick Douglass and Nelson Mandela (all just as stimulating here as they had been on earth!)—to lesser-known, obscure holy ones whose lives the world had never fully recognized. And all seemed part of a warm, caring, harmonious, buoyant family. Perhaps those nineteenth-century utopias like Charles Fourier's phalansteries or the villages of cooperation of Robert Owen actually were within reach.[22]

---

19. O'Hear and O'Hear, *Picturing the Apocalypse*, 231 and plate 3.
20. Kovacs and Rowland, *Revelation*, 235–36.
21. Cyprian of Carthage, *Letters, Volume III*, 67. Cf. Catholic Church, *Catechism*, 268.
22. Heilbroner, *Worldly Philosophers*, 106–21.

Then I heard myself ask, "How can these things be?" Everyone deferred to that exuberant traveler, the Apostle Paul, who discoursed with gusto on the glory of the celestial and the glory of the terrestrial, emphatically expounding on the nature of the resurrection body (1 Cor. 15:35–49). Our physical body is but a tent, or garment, for the ego, or soul. After death, God will prepare for us a new garment, just as Jesus' perishable body took on what was imperishable (2 Cor. 5:1–5).[23] We will no longer be dominated by our lower natures; instead, "wherever the spirit wills," says Augustine, "there, in a flash, will the body be."[24] Anselm characterized our resurrected bodies in terms of "agility" (i.e., the ability to move immediately from one point to another since God is everywhere), "penetrability" (i.e., the ability to pass through solid matter since all things are of God), and "perpetuity" (e.g., the ability to live forever since all times are in God).[25] Perhaps we will even "be able to live under water like fish," speculated Renaissance humanist Lorenzo Valla.[26] The soul is not entombed in, but endowed with, a body—for we are body-soul complexes.[27] This has similarities to Lucian's Island of the Blessed, where naked souls—without flesh or substance—walk about in what seem to be real bodies, yet turn out to be tinted shadows. People never grow old, but remain the same age as when they first arrived.[28] By contrast, in New Jerusalem residents can travel faster than the speed of light, visit remote stars in the twinkling of an eye, are nourished by the waters and trees of life, experience the five senses to a degree unknown on earth, and even communicate via empathic telepathy. Thus, in *Paradiso* 26:103–108, Adam actually reads Dante's thoughts, since they are reflected in "that truthful mirror," the mind of God.[29]

Not only did I find physical deformities healed, but debilitating mental conditions as well. Whatever the last state of the body on earth, whether decomposed, burned, or devoured, it was resurrected pristine.[30] Early church historian Eusebius relates how the second-century martyrs

---

23. McDannell and Lang, *Heaven: A History*, 35.
24. Augustine, *City of God (Abridged)*, 541.
25. Russell, *A History of Heaven*, 115.
26. Valla, *On Pleasure*, 303. Cf. McDannell and Lang, *Heaven: A History*, 128.
27. Kirk, *Vision of God*, 384–85.
28. Lucian, *Selected Satires*, 38.
29. Boersma, *Seeing God*, 223.
30. Russell, *A History of Heaven*, 87.

in Lyons were mutilated and burned during a time of persecution in order that "they shall have no hope of the resurrection." When their ashes were thrown into the Rhone, bystanders taunted, "Now let us see if they rise again, and if their god can help them."[31] But how foolish, reckoned Methodius of Olympus, since our resurrection body is simply a "rearrangement" of its original constituents—just as a statue melted down can be recast from the same material, this time, however, without blemish or defect.[32] Cappadocian father Gregory of Nyssa conjectured that on the day of the resurrection, our body's scattered atoms will remember one another and, like the dispersed children of Israel, reassemble at God's command.[33] Marks of torture on the bodies of martyrs will, in glory, shine like badges of honor (beauty marks, if you will), avowed Ephraim of Syria, among others, much like those nail holes in Jesus' own hands and feet.[34] Expanding on his earlier views, Augustine concluded that our spiritual bodies will consist of flesh and bones just like Christ's, capable of being both perceived and touched.[35]

Heaven, as Origen supposed, is a kind of university for those who are anxious to unravel the universe's enigmas.[36] Here Plato's ideal becomes real, since in contemplating God we meditate on absolute good. The perfect knowledge Aristotle had so desired is attainable, since we no longer need to receive information piecemeal, but can grasp a unified overall pattern.[37] What better place to pursue further studies, since our instructor has both absolute knowledge and infinite patience?[38] Indeed, eighteenth-century hymn writer Isaac Watts believed that saints will be "most delightfully engaged in recounting to each other the wondrous steps of providence, wisdom and mercy." They may explore "various and different globes," then share their "millions of new discoveries of divine

31. Eusebius, *History of the Church*, 236. Cf. McDannell and Lang, *Heaven: A History*, 49.

32. McGrath, *A Brief History of Heaven*, 34–35.

33. Zaleski and Zaleski, *Book of Heaven*, 374. St. Gregory of Nyssa, *On the Soul and Resurrection*, 107, 117.

34. Russell, *A History of Heaven*, 79.

35. Augustine, *The Retractions*, 74–76. Cf. McDannell and Lang, *Heaven: A History*, 61.

36. Trigg, *Origen: The Bible and Philosophy*, 115. Cf. Origen, *On First Principles*, 186–92.

37. Harris, "State of the Dead (Christian)," 834.

38. McDannell and Lang, *Heaven: A History*, 297.

power" with their fellows. After all, "when a blessed spirit has dwelt in heaven a thousand years, and conversed with God, Christ, angels, and fellow-spirits, . . . shall it know nothing more of the nature and wondrous properties of God than it knew the first moment of its arrival there?"[39]

The Enlightenment philosopher Leibniz maintained, "I feel that restless activity is an essential part of the happiness of creatures;" "there must be a continuous and uninterrupted progress toward even greater good."[40] In all likelihood, in heaven we will hold official positions, contends C.S. Lewis, ruling over cities (Lk. 19:17–19), judging angels (1 Cor. 6:3.), serving as pillars in God's temple (Rev. 3:12).[41] God will assign us tasks, asserts Isaac Watts.[42] Activists will perform astounding feats, administer mighty estates, spread the knowledge of God everywhere, while contemplatives will experience multi-dimensional visions of peace. Yet no one will ever grow tired. There will be no doctor-prescribed rest and recuperation, since all will pace themselves according to the rhythms of the eternal Sabbath, which Augustine labeled "an eighth day."[43] So often in this world our labors lead to anguish, stress, and alienation. In the next life though, nineteenth-century American pastor David Gregg believed, we will be "as free from care and toil and fatigue as is the wing-stroke of the jubilant lark when it soars into the sunlight of a fresh, clear day and, spontaneously and for self-relief, pours out its thrilling carol."[44] "Then we shall live in our own element," Puritan divine Richard Baxter supposed. "We are now as the fish in a vessel of water, only so much as will keep them alive; but what is that to the ocean? We have a little air let in to us, to afford us breathing; but what is that to the sweet and fresh gales upon mount Sion? We have a beam of the sun to lighten our darkness, and a warm ray to keep us from freezing; but then we shall live in its light and be revived by its heat for ever."[45] As Isaiah prophesied, "For the earth will be full of the knowledge of the Lord as the waters cover the sea," (Isa 11:9).

---

39. Watts, *Works*, Volume 2, 173, 174, 177. Cf. McDannell and Lang, *Heaven: A History*, 209.

40. McDannell and Lang, *Heaven: A History*, 277. Cf. "Principles of Nature and of Grace," Leibniz, *Philosophical Writings*, 203–4.

41. Lewis, *Weight of Glory*, 7

42. Watts, *Works*, Volume 2, 173.

43. Augustine, *City of God*, 1091.

44. Gregg, *The Heaven-Life*, 62. Cf. McDannell and Lang, *Heaven: A History*, 282.

45. Baxter, *Saints' Everlasting Rest*, 31–32.

We will learn when and how our own faith journey unfolded. "There, our Lord will reveal . . . great secrets," predicted seventeenth-century bishop of Geneva Francis de Sales. He will speak to believers "of his suffering and of what else he has done for them. He will tell them: In such a time I have suffered this for you. He will explain to them the mystery of his incarnation, salvation, and redemption, saying: I was waiting for you so long, running after you when you were stubborn, and with a gentle violence I forced you to receive my grace." "I gave you at such a moment such an impulse and such an inspiration, I used such a person to draw you to myself."[46] All the bewildering pieces of life's puzzle will fall into place.

"But what of the memories?" I wondered. "What of our previous sins and that suffocating sense of guilt?" Bonaventure and Thomas Aquinas discoursed on the beatific vision which takes away pain. Via divine rapture we wean ourselves from focusing on the self. "The memory of our previous miseries will be a matter of purely mental contemplation," remarked Augustine, quoting from his *City of God*, "with no renewal of any feelings connected with these experiences"—much in the way a doctor diagnoses a patient's symptoms without having to undergo the disease itself.[47] In Samuel Johnson's fictional happy valley, the hero Rasselas moaned, "I fear pain when I do not feel it; I sometimes shrink at evils recollected; and sometimes start at evils anticipated."[48] But glory be to God, in heaven our phobias, manias, neuroses, and traumas will be purged by that healing balm in Gilead, our feverish minds calmed. No longer will we experience what Cicero called *unguis in ulcere*, that accusing knife which keeps our wounds open and bleeding.[49]

Those age-old enemies of humanity—pain, loss, and death—will have been overcome once-and-for-all. "There shall be no more crying, nor sorrow; for he that is owner of the place will wipe all tears from our eyes," Christian tells Pliable in Bunyan's *Pilgrim's Progress*, in a reference to Revelation 21:4.[50] "O healthful place, where none are sick! O fortunate land, where all are kings! O holy assembly, where all are priests! How free a state, where none are servants, but to their supreme Monarch!" exclaims Richard Baxter. "The poor man shall no more be tired with his

---

46. McDannell and Lang, *Heaven: A History*, 165.
47. Augustine, *City of God (Abridged)*, 542.
48. Johnson, *Rasselas, Poems, and Selected Prose*, 611.
49. Mawson, *Dictionary of Foreign Terms*, 347.
50. Bunyan, *Pilgrim's Progress*, 56.

labors: no more hunger or thirst, cold or nakedness: no pinching frosts or scorching heats. Our faces shall no more be pale or sad; no more breaches in friendship, nor parting of friends asunder; no more trouble accompanying our relations, nor voice of lamentation heard in our dwellings."[51] Jerusalem will become what it was always meant to be, "the city of peace." Heaven will be the converse of earthly tribulation, for there purity reigns, not pollution; justice, not oppression; security, not dread; abundance, not want. "There are none of those waves in that harbor, which now so toss us up and down," continues Baxter. "Today we are well, tomorrow sick; today in esteem, tomorrow in disgrace; today we have friends, tomorrow none."[52] "Because they had followed in the footsteps God had shown," Hildegard of Bingen imagined in an allegorical vision concerning the holy virgins in Paradise, "they wore foot coverings that shone through, as if they had been taken from the fountain of living water."[53] As Zechariah had prophesied, God will be a wall of fire in latter-day Jerusalem, and his immortal glory will become a tabernacle in its midst (Zech. 2:5).[54]

All shall "see" Christ (Rev. 22:4). But what will he look like? John of Patmos, using charged symbolic language, noticed "one like the Son of Man" in the midst of seven lamp stands; he wore a long robe with a golden sash across his chest, holding seven stars in his right hand. His head and hair were white as wool or snow, his eyes like a flame of fire, his feet like burnished bronze, his voice like the sound of many waters, his face as bright as the sun—while a double-edged sword protruded from his mouth (Rev. 1:12–16).[55] Elsewhere, Christ appears as a lamb who was slaughtered, having seven horns and seven eyes (5:6). When heaven is opened, John beholds Christ, now crowned, riding a white horse, who is leading the armies of heaven. His eyes were like flames of fire and his robe dipped in blood. From his mouth comes forth a sword to smite the nations; he will rule with a rod of iron. He is referred to as "The Word of God"—on his robe and thigh are inscribed "King of kings and Lord of lords." He is called "Faithful and True" and has a secret name no one knows except himself (Rev. 19:11–16).[56] (In the twelfth-century Seldon

---

51. Baxter, *Saints' Everlasting Rest*, 35–36.
52. Baxter, *Saints' Everlasting Rest*, 32.
53. Hildegard of Bingen, *Book of the Rewards of Life*, 282.
54. Beale, *Revelation*, 475.
55. Beal, *The Book of Revelation*, 13.
56. Beal, *The Book of Revelation*, 26.

Apocalypse, we see an actual sword projecting from Christ's mouth.[57]) He announces, "I am the root and descendant of David, the bright morning star" (Rev. 22:16). His name is on his followers' foreheads for they belong to him forever (Rev. 22:4), much in the way "Holy to the Lord" was written on a rosette and placed on the turban of Israel's high priest (Ex. 28:36–38).[58]

We, freed from our shackles, "without needing any figure, riddle or parable," declared fifth-century Cyril of Alexandria, "shall contemplate, as it were with face uncovered and unencumbered mind, the beauty of the divine nature of our God and Father."[59] But how? In ways beyond our present understanding, the glorified body will be adapted to beholding.[60] "And so I say that the saints will see God *in* the body;" Augustine surmised, "but whether they will see *through* the eyes of the body, in the same way we now see the sun, moon, stars, sea and earth and all things on the earth—that is no easy question."[61] We shall certainly recognize Christ, and be overjoyed, for we will see him as he is, being glorified just as he is (1 John 3:2). In fact, the Eastern Orthodox have sought to envision heaven for centuries by gazing on icons like Andrei Rublov's "The Savior," created in fifteenth-century Zvenigorod, with that enigmatic face and brown, piercing eyes.[62]

Then it dawned on me that I was totally engulfed by God. He extended as far and as high as the city's limits, yet could not be contained by them, and he it was that held the molecules of my body together. Somehow he was at the center of all of the thoughts and acts of everyone I encountered. Life flowed out from the Triune God and then glowingly returned. "For while we carry on our present life in many different ways, there are many things in which we participate, such as time, air, place, food and drink, clothing, sun, lamplight, and many other necessities of life," asserts Gregory of Nyssa, "of which none is God. The blessedness which we await, however, does not need any of these, but the divine

---

57. Hind, *Faces of God*, 162.

58. Beale, *Revelation*, 503.

59. Kelly, *Early Christian Doctrines*, 487. Cf. Stewart & Thomas, trans. & eds., *John*, 500.

60. Oden, *Life in the Spirit*, 461–62.

61. Augustine, *City of God*, 1082.

62. Hind, *Faces of God*, 155.

nature will become everything for us and will replace everything."[63] As the Beatitudes insist, the pure in heart will see God (Mt. 5:8).

Puritan divine Thomas Watson says that when the saints behold the brightness of God's majesty, they shall obtain "a tincture of that glory."[64] The redeemed will become celestial luminaries (Dan. 12:3, Matt. 13:43). Scholar Jeffrey Burton Russell has compared this to weaving, where each thread lovingly touches another, until the entire web shines like a field of stars.[65] Yes, God will make our bodies shine (*splendere*). We will be "filled with sight of God shining gloriously around us as it once shone for the disciples at the divine transfiguration," taught Pseudo-Dionysius, "and somehow, in a way we cannot know, we shall be united with him, and our understanding carried away, blessedly happy, we shall be struck by his blazing light."[66] Perhaps those luminous, phantasmagoric, ethereal saints in El Greco's paintings, such as "St. John's Vision of the Apocalypse," give us an inkling of how this could look.[67]

In *Paradiso* 29:12-18, Beatrice looks directly at that point of light, God, in whom every *where* (*ubi*) and every *when* (*quando*) are concentrated. God has even gone so far as to make reflections—immaterial spirits of angels—which are so like him that they can affirm, "I, too, exist."[68] Gender itself seems to have no ultimate, eschatological significance, for in heaven there will be no marrying or giving in marriage (Lk. 20:34-36).[69] Near the end of *The Divine Comedy*, Dante watches a single light turn into three circles, each of a different color, yet equal in magnitude. "The first," he notes, "seemed to reflect the next like rainbow on rainbow, and the third was like a flame equally breathed forth by the other two."[70] In one of those circles he perceived a human form.[71] He then concludes his poem by exalting that eternal love which moves the universe, synchronizing our wills to our desires (*Paradiso*, 33:143-45.)

---

63. Gregory of Nyssa, *On Soul and the Resurrection*, 86.
64. Watson, *The Beatitudes*, 121. Cf. Boersma, *Seeing God*, 418-19.
65. Russell, *A History of Heaven*, 6.
66. "The Divine Names," Pseudo-Dionysius, *The Complete Works*, 52-53. Cf. Russell, *A History of Heaven*, 79, 93.
67. Puppi, *El Greco*, 19-20.
68. Gallagher, *To Hell and Back*, 190.
69. Boersma, *Seeing God*, 425.
70. Zaleski, "When I Get to Heaven," 31.
71. Canto 33: 115-120, 130-31, Dante, *Divine Comedy: Paradiso*, 379.

New Jerusalem is the bride, the perfected community of Christ's body, as each member's joy lights up every other's, in an unending chain reaction. "I saw faces all given to love, adorned by the light of Another, and by their own smile," writes Dante in *Paradiso* 31:49–50.[72] What was the happiest day of your life? Happiness on earth has always been dogged by the gnawing awareness that it never lasts. "In this city all the citizens will be immortal," announces Augustine, "for human beings will obtain that which the angels have never lost."[73] "In meeting the light," extols Flemish mystic John Ruusbroec, "the heart experiences so much delight and pleasure that it cannot contain itself but bursts out in a cry of joy." Just as, on earth, the heart swam "in a state of bliss" whenever it encountered God; far transcending these experiences will be the teeming, rapturous delights of heaven.[74] At that festive banquet in Lucian's Elysian Field, there were two flowing springs, one of laughter and one of joy; all guests were to drink of each.[75] Think of Beethoven's Symphony No. 9, with its rousing "Ode to Joy," adapted from Schiller: "*Ahndest du den Schöpfer, Welt?/ Such ihn* überm *Sternenzelt!*" ("Do you know the creator, world?/ Seek him high beyond all stars.")[76] You, too, can join that chorus the morning stars began at the dawn of creation (Job. 38:6–7).

Will our spiritual hunger ever be satiated? No. Finite creatures can never fully comprehend God or encompass all that he is. We will never know God to the extent he knows himself. Thus Gregory of Nyssa held to a doctrine of *epektasis*, or "eternal progress," a term borrowed from Philippians 3:13.[77] Our vision is a "falling inward" into God, as the mind moves from glory to glory, from height to height, since there is no limit to how many peaks one may scale. Imagine standing on the shore of an ocean and straining your eyes to the distant horizon. Once you sail to that point, you find the horizon still farther off. So God is like a sea with no end. In terms of spiritual growth, every place we arrive, insisted Gregory, is but a new point of departure, for in the next world ongoing progress is the law of spiritual life.[78] The more eagerly we pursue virtue, the greater

---

72. Dante, *Divine Comedy: Paradiso*, 351.
73. Augustine, *City of God*, 1022.
74. Ruusbroec, *Spiritual Espousals*, 87–89. Cf. McGrath, *Brief History of Heaven*, 142.
75. Lucian, *Selected Satires*, 39.
76. Burk, "Symphony in D Minor, No. 9," 68.
77. Danielou, ed., *From Glory to Glory*, 58.
78. Baxter, *Introduction to Christian Mysticism*, 88–89.

will be our capacity for love. The greater our capacity for love, the more we shall see God. Gregory rhapsodizes, "For this is truly perfection: never to stop growing towards what is better and never placing any limit on perfection."[79] What a heavenly virtuous circle. Alleluia! It is impossible for God to ever fully gratify our soul's desires, since he always has more beauty in reserve. While he is eager to reveal himself completely, we can absorb him only in stages.[80] There is always one more rung to ascend on Jacob's celestial ladder.

What of the marriage supper of the Lamb and the eternal dance? In a midrash by Rabbi Akiba, "The letter *kaf* [whose name means 'palm of the hand'] indicates that at the banquet of the pious in the World to Come, he [God] will clap his hands in great joy, and will rise and dance before them at the banquet. And each . . . will be accompanied by . . . myriad myriads of ministering angels, with pillars of lightning round about them and sparks of splendor will surround them, and fireworks of radiance will make their faces glow and sparks of light will make their eyelids shine."[81] As master of ceremonies, God leads the cosmic revelry as heaven undergoes continuous re-invigoration.[82] In Fra Angelico's painting *The Last Judgment*, there is a round dance of humans and angels, "The Dance of the Blessed"—nearby, we see an angel and a friar embrace.[83] "Yea, angels as well as saints will be our blessed acquaintances," affirms Richard Baxter. "Those who now are willingly our ministering spirits, will willingly then be our companions in joy."[84] Similarly, we note in Virgil's vision of the Elysian Fields, some "were treading a rhythmic dance and as they danced they sang. And there, too, was Orpheus the Thracian seer attired in his trailing gown, who answered their rhythm on seven intervals of notes, striking out the melody, now with fingers or now, over again, with an ivory quill," while others were "feasting and singing a joyful hymn of praise."[85]

Plato, in *Phaedrus*, said that the universe, and all beings in it, long to return to the One.[86] The entire cosmos is summed up in and conjoined

---

79. Saint Gregory of Nyssa, *Ascetical Works*, 122.
80. Baxter, *Introduction to Christian Mysticism*, 91.
81. Patai, *Messiah Texts*, 242.
82. Vaus, *Mere Theology*, 211.
83. McDannell and Lang, *Heaven: A History*, 128–31.
84. Baxter, *Saints' Everlasting Rest*, 30.
85. Virgil, *Aeneid*, 166–67.
86. Russell, *A History of Heaven*, 20. Cf. Hackforth, "Phaedrus," 495.

to the Christian Godhead, from Alpha to Omega, where, as Paul puts it in 1 Corinthians 15:28, all will be in all. In *Paradiso* 33:85–87, Dante declares, "I saw ingathered, bound by love in one single volume, that which is dispersed in leaves throughout the universe."[87] Indeed, everything within us shouts that there must be something more; the searing struggles of life can't simply have been for naught. "In fact," writes Thomas Aquinas, "it would seem stupid for a person to make a very strong instrument to be used for a short hour and then discard it completely."[88] We, and all of creation, groan inwardly, eagerly awaiting our full redemption (Rom. 8:22–23) and the unveiling of God's ongoing purposes. "Your soul has a curious shape," hypothesized C.S. Lewis, "because it is a hollow made to fit a particular swelling in the infinite contours of the divine substance, or a key to unlock one of the doors in the house with many mansions.... Your place in heaven will seem to be made for you and you alone, because you were made for it—made for it stitch by stitch as a glove is made for a hand."[89] No wonder, when the unicorn in Lewis' *The Last Battle* arrives at the new Narnia, it shouts, "I have come home at last! This is my real country! I belong here. This is the land I have been looking for all my life."[90]

This new Garden of Eden will be a *reformatio in melius* (a "reformation for the better"), claims Augustine.[91] Throughout *The Divine Comedy*, Dante referred to his guide as Beatrice, a name derived from *beata* or "blessed"—she is a metaphor of the restoration of human nature to a state even more perfect than its first.[92] "All that is true, honorable, just, pure, pleasing, and commendable in the whole of creation ... is gathered up in the future city of God—renewed, re-created, boosted to its highest glory,"[93] advises modern Dutch theologian Herman Bavinck. As the saying goes, "you ain't seen nothin' yet." In fact, near the end of the Book of Revelation, God proclaims, "See, I am making all things new" (Rev. 21:5). Twentieth-century Jewish author Isaac Bashevis Singer once called creativity, the "highest divine attribute" for "God is eternally in Genesis."[94]

87. Dante, *Divine Comedy: Paradiso*, 377.
88. *Exposition of Job*, chapter 14, lecture 5, Bourke, ed., *Pocket Aquinas*, 362.
89. Lewis, *Problem of Pain*, 147–48.
90. Lewis, *Last Battle*, 162.
91. Russell, *History of Heaven*, 85
92. Russell, *History of Heaven*, 152.
93. Bavinck, *Reformed Dogmatics*, 720. Cf. Boersma, *Seeing God*, 38–39.
94. Singer, *Love and Exile*, 153. Cf. Parrinder, *Dictionary of Religious & Spiritual Quotations*, 39.

In heaven, observes C.S. Lewis, there will be a freshness each "morning;" each "day" will seem like a new sunrise.[95] Allah will pose one last question to believers in Paradise, according to Muslim thinker Said Hammád b. Sulaimán, "Have I fulfilled the promises I made to you in the world, or have I come short of them in any way?"[96]

Then my vision vanished and I found myself asleep at my desk. Staring down at exquisite diagrams and unearthly conversations, I took my notes and tossed them into the fire, for my time had not yet come.

In this brief fantasy I have pieced together verses from Scripture along with concepts from major thinkers, primarily Christian, throughout the ages, comparing them to texts in other religions. As Paul says, we now see in a mirror dimly, but then we will see God face to face (1 Cor. 13:12). If, from your perspective, my vision of heaven is not that exhilarating or enticing, why not add a few touches of your own? What do you think will be the ultimate in fulfillment for those who are good, holy, and righteous? If I asked you to paint a portrait of a virtuous heaven, what other mellifluous features might you include?

---

95. Lewis, *Great Divorce*, 34–35, 112. Cf. Vaus, *Mere Theology*, 212.
96. Jeffery, ed., *Islam: Muhammad and His Religion*, 99

A Day Like No Other

A day to rend one's heart,
when rivers bubble, mountains seethe,
formerly dormant cones splash the evening skies.

Land creatures evolve poisoned spines,
aristocratic mammals are decimated by freak viruses,
phosphorescent fish bathe in neutrino seas.

The moon hides behind her kimono curtain,
great portents flare-expand, are sucked to pieces,
the sun near collapses, spiral galaxies reverse their spin.

Left- and right-handed ions turn ambidextrous,
bipolar gravity attracts-repulses,
the secret nucleus is born of anti-matter.

Time loses its momentum, motion disperses,
there's a brief respite between the heaves of storm;
and a still, small snail leaves her posterior talus trail.

Deceitful Time

Deceitful time,
cruel as the unwelcome scythe
when the tree is bursting fruit,
time hath dominion and reigns
o'er every prelate and usurper's crown,
we beat our ceramic heads against its wheel.

Facial powders, mascara, hidden snaps
corral in time's oozing flesh,
the miser and the spendthrift
both feel her inexorable poker hand,
despite their staunchest efforts,
Dutchmen are still rounding that elusive cape.

Time rusts, creases, and corrodes,
obeys the second law of entropy—nothing new can stay—
shiny, flashing, climate-controlled,
ur-original, or even approximate mint,
pristine equilibrium is shaken
by consecutive experimental -isms.

Time wounds all that's masterpiece,
removes the pulpit from the sanctuary to the street,
stains courtesans with blemishes and warts,
uncontrollable time like some knight errant
vanquishes flapping windmills,
deflates even the likes of Priam, Hector, and Aeneas.

All Is Smoke

All is smoke,
a vibration, barely an echo,
the past—hazy,
the future—shrouded,
even today
seems like a Dakota blizzard,
my life is
a puff of vapor
—nothing substantial lasts.

Even the evergreen
throws off its needles,
the sequoia is felled by lightning bolts,
our cambium rings
display accelerating/decelerating growth,
worlds break apart,
islands slip forever
beneath uncharted waves,
jeweled manuscripts are lost.

Barbarians ride in,
attack fortified palaces,
intermarry, then are heard of no more,
remnants, shards, debris
deteriorate in mausoleums,
artifacts lie buried in unexhumed graves,
the immortality we sought
trickles away,
our ancestral clan titles vanish.

Under non-deceptive *qodesh* light
our much-vaunted righteousness
appears as filthy, polluted rags.

Time Is . . . .

Time is, time was, time shall be no more,
footfalls pace and pace,
an orphan girl hands me her shooting stars,
a connoisseur of wine vomits on the Bowery steps,
Zurván doubts: good and evil hatch
from a doppelgänger shell,
Kairos grafted onto *Chronos*' bud,
"*Panta rhei.*"

When I learned to tie my shoes,
the hobgoblins could pinpoint blame,
sinewy hands knead encephalon dough,
memory categorizes cryptograms,
fashions baobabs on asteroid B-612,
a verifiable fact juts out
like the plum in Adam's neck,
a hydraulus among Hero's pneumatic toys,
a Mayan captive flayed by an Aztec rite.

Time's irreversible lock, a silver iodide blip,
theoretically one could sightsee on all the galaxies
—185,299+ miles per second—
and be cremated on every planet's ashes,
the apotheosis of Hercules or Joseph Merrick,
the stars groan sympathetically before a ragamuffin brain.

Like waking from a dream and surrendering
to hypnosis or Mesmer's magnetism,
though I be as patient as Penelope
and twice as cunning as her late bard,

under Saturn I'll revolve in the fifth ring,
beyond the moon Erik the Red's a manticore
and eiderdown pillows are stuffed with angels' wings,
a caesium pendulum is placed within the Greenwich mean
and a universe of flute holes stopped up at eclipse time.

We are the gouged-out sockets creeping up the psychedelic stair,
like Joyce and Milton we hear the luminescent dial,
but can't see the switch,
or like Philomela we gawk without our tongue,
or bob like Tantalus, yet die of dehydration.

The Whining Mandolin

The whining mandolin
sobs out tales of a shipwrecked heart,
I have been buffeted by tsunamis, spouts,
nearly drowned in Leviathan's wake,
been torn apart by coral cacti,
drifted in vertigo beneath a blue, nihilistic sky,
where it was futile to hoist a flimsy sail
or to tack toward an azimuth-less horizon.

Dazed, I thought swordfish were harpooning the bow,
barnacle mutants puncturing the metallic hull,
monstrous squids tossing the schooner about like an air-filled balloon,
a blue whale nearly inhaled the crew while sniffing plankton.

Where are you, my serene Tahitian lagoon
that I might Gauguin-introduce post-Impressionism,
instead, I inadvertently fashioned a cradle of spikes and nails,
when all I wanted was to make whoopee with the sea sprites.

The Dance of Death

Macabre skeletons doing a jig,
pope and pauper adorned the same,
demons plucking out souls by the bushel basket,
Munch-like scream—all to no avail.

Innocent IV, Charlemagne,
troubadours and courtly ladies,
churches turned to sewers,
St. John Lateran's brothel.

Millennia of installments,
now the final payment is due,
naked of accumulation,
ripped from banquets and carnal ecstasy.

Serves notice of the omnipotence of time,
sand drips inexorably,
pendulum swings on those with double lives
or brings the curtain down on incomplete performances.

Cerberus growls, ferryman wants his fare,
a feather's weighing of the heart,
Mot consumes the whole
kit and caboodle.

Milquetoast souls
reluctant to leave an ass,
Gothic terrors make this world
an Abaddon of guilty apprehension.
Funeral march in somber black-and-white,

contorted eyes, noses out of joint,
bodies of abrupt angles,
ears and flesh in cinders.

Kaleidoscope of the seven virtues
interrupted by the scorching truth,
the vulture, kite, and sparrowhawk,
stinking corpses draw demi-flies.

Rattling bones, tapdancing marionettes,
plagues and kingly duels
bring their half a legion,
famines put them over.

Not the loneliness of existential hells,
but the squalor of urban slums,
not individual knightly warriors,
but cartloads of conformity.

Orphans, beggars shoveled in indifferently,
unction recited in archaic tongues,
masses to shorten purgatory,
relics seeking to procure the homicide's release.

Feudal lords wedding Lady Poverty,
damsels in extreme distress,
dust lost to amorphous sod,
a casket containing amino acids worth a pittance.

God, the only animating force
in this hermetically-sealed universe,
he wound it up—
only to watch man bring it to judgment.

Delusion

Invincible Müntzer
catching cannonballs
on his beheaded sleeves.

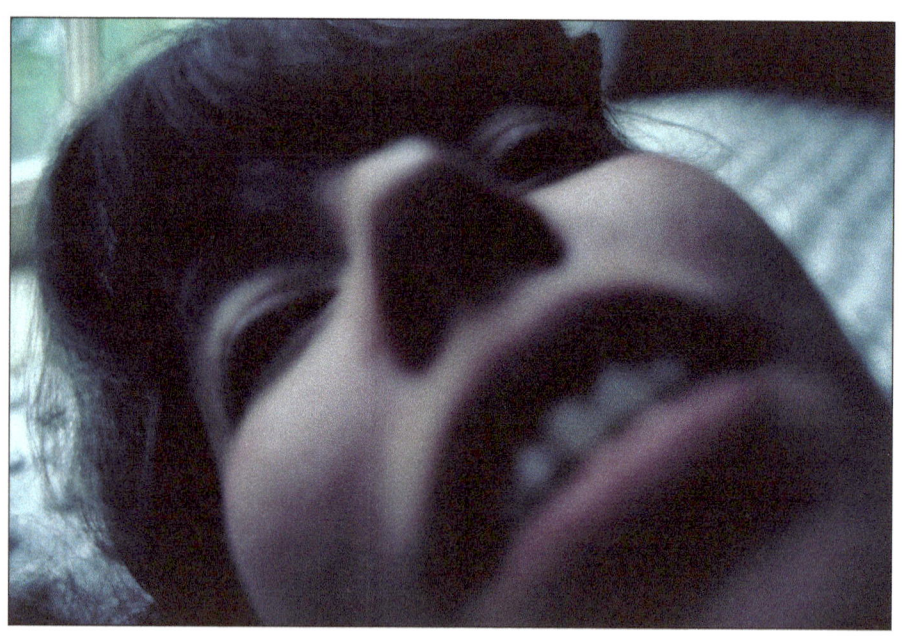

A Night of Peacock Eyes

The night is full of peacock eyes
which engulf our slippery souls,
like a vaporous cloud of predators who stare out
from behind unobtrusive trunks and branches,
all is hushed anticipation
as each ascertains the weak, the sickly, the aged,
far from neon strobes and Edison lamps
death glints out from parabolic reflectors.

Here only a curtain of fog could usher in peace,
a warped mirror merely elongates the odds,
nightmares stalk in Technicolor,
muted shadows howl and scream,
what's nearby is disturbing,
what's further away is still more objectionable,
black envelopes the legions of radiance
like a gnawing, insidious dawn,
angels and demons clash over Moses' corpse,
desiring to dispose of his mellifluous, perfumed bones.

Will insanity fly up and perch
in the extended roots of the banyan,
stall like an occluded front,
dooming us to monsoon downpour and despair,
while above, ever-circling spheres pour forth their crackling Muzak?
Shall I pledge you my troth,
submit my acrid eyes and heart
to warmed-over, Molotov passions?

Sleep is a fatal shell, cast it off;
be alert, ever-watchful, enter into that land of changing splendors;
we sought to kindle fire on earth,
now it smells of dormant embers,
the reeds acted as snorkels
for those without bladder or gills,
I'm weary from uninterrupted dreams,
my horizon suffocated by flaccid assumptions,
the foliage closes in like a green, implacable wall,
the bushes resemble churlish elves
which titter ring-around-the-rosie.

No solvent could ever wash away our stains,
guilt clings like a mythical fall,
where is vaunted redemption
when earth and sky bubble up viscously in a cauldron?
the slopes, the glens, the pastures
appear emerald as Eire's shamrock,
yet still I'm led by the nose
by those three enchanted sisters—the world, the flesh, the devil.

Return, return, o Shulammite,
from your spiced bed to this lilied cavern,
having wandered through the copious undergrowth of aphrodisiac blossoms
toward some gossamer, ethereal sea,
I, who escaped adolescence into Arcady,
can still discern the angry clamor of cymbals,
my lungs wheeze like a fitful respirator,
should I seek to pluck the highest, most succulent pears,
my outsized grasp dissipates.

So, if you please, neutralize these plutonium hands,
which usher all into the chasm of your presence,
I feel a soothing balm of purgation
as excesses and abominations are irradiated,

glowing tendrils trope toward fathomless eternity;
meanwhile, I, who have fallen under the spell of a healing Asclepius,
took a gulp from his peculiar Lethe potion
and became what I had never been.

The Reluctant Left Hand of My God

Partial, gibbous, and eventually full,
the wrath of God's persistence:
my cares, heavyweight half-pennies,
my piety, deluded common sense,
my prayers, self-hypnosis,
my ambition, counter-drive.

My mind, reveries and lost causes,
arteries awash with decaying red blood cells,
oxygen-deprived, the platelet count is low,
white corpuscles refuse to take up arms,
virus infects the nooks and crannies of my pancreas.

Unsound judgment,
raging acerbic wit,
venial indiscretions,
sparks of "it might have been,"
the mercy seat is silent.

Gaping absolution,
penitence half-said,
I call God to be my witness,
the blood does not always purify.

Sometimes it corrodes my ducts,
wrenches my insides,
beckons me to a defendant's seat
where my Advocate is my Judge.

Discipline: the reluctant left hand of my God,
Michael is foreman of the jury,
the angels deliberate their 12 chunks of truth—
but can be overruled for an ill-considered verdict.

Sentence meted out with no malice or predilection,
law of karma, *lex talionis*,
a flurry of plea bargaining,
more often justice and mercy kiss behind the screen,
radical common grace.

"There Was Silence..."

There was silence in heaven for the space of half an hour,
when God collected his Sabbath thoughts,
time intersected eternity's diameter,
the gates of ivory and horn were loosed upon the dreaming world,
angels slipped incorporeal through our layered atmosphere
as psychokinetic fingers pushed forward the plot,
and every self-determining oscilloscope went awry.

Ebbinghaus grasped memory's crazy fluctuations,
if we submit to the magnetizer's pure will, our insomnia escapes,
seeing the future as vivid as Frederica Hauffe's bubble,
I glimpsed perpetuity when I walked along the shore,
silence plummets and crawls through the holes in our umbrella,
like prisoners in the tower we whittle away on ivory guillotines,
free fall outside the reach of even the Red, Blue, and Yellow Buddhas.

The Meaning Flowed On

Jarred out of syntax,
the meaning continued to flow,
multi-dimensional as the primal ether,
immeasurable except by polyrhythmic beats or jams,
like turgid salts which leak out of their viscous envelope
into a free-floating, atomized
mysticism uncolored by mere containers;
currents were dispersed within secondary, tertiary
vortices and pools.

I tried to extrapolate the linear sequence,
mix in known periodic elements
in precise, quantifiable proportions,
but the sum wouldn't add up,
unexpected subtleties intervened,
the cohesive bonds couldn't be reliably monitored,
strange neutrinos played havoc with the spectral lines,
fluids evaporated, solids liquified,
a mysterious precipitate remained.

But the significance gained momentum
as it pressed toward a vanishing point on the far horizon,
so I strung together chain-length refutations,
adding here an ingenuous remark, there a bold conjecture,
—these couldn't be overturned by a single contradictory wobble—
the ball bearings rolled haphazardly within their hollow tubing,
and I have yet to close up those dilated pupils.

On a June Evening

The field is swathed with blinking fireflies,
the moon is luminous as a flaming orchid,
starbursts twitter all along the blackened canvas,
constellations swirl up dizzily from antique horizons.

Are we morose, condemned to sublunar pain,
while orbs circle about the rarefied fifth element,
unheeding of mutability or egregious stares?
Has some penultimate catastrophe of galactic proportions
undermined our brittle brashness,
we who are never secure five furlongs from home?

I hesitate, I stammer, I lisp and limp,
wobbling along a borderless periphery, the shores of indecision,
unstable as a periodic yo-yo which half enters our solar system,
 and is half caught up in some other dimension,
turning to and fro like a fluctuating gyroscope
caught in a cosmic, existential quagmire.

Strange rustlings I hear, odd hoots, out-of-this-world howls,
jarred from my sedentary reverie by nearby realities
which can gouge or maim or kill,
then surrounded by amillennial, interplanetary visions,
I pull out a smoking .45
and blow romance to smithereens.

"Nichts als Mauern"[1]

Nothing but canyons and walls
which stare across cool, synthetic pavement:
steel sequoia, angle-iron cactus,
translucent domes of riveted polymer,
street balustrades resemble cast-iron fireflies,
diesel behemoths belch in underground caverns,
blind termites peer out, their antennae crumpled,
the *douloi*—undercounted by societal engineers.

Mesa Verde high-rises, robotic living spaces,
Neo-Gothic spires dominated by obelisks to finance,
radios out-blare any known noise squelchers,
drug wackos collapse like epileptics from syringe overdoses,
to beg for one's bread means getting jostled, pummeled,
limousine millionaires sweep past in the grand style of chauffeured anonymity,
hustlers briskly strut out from assembly line showrooms.

The lingua franca: Pidgin English,
a hawker flips char-black burgers, green brassieres are the Irish fashion,
in parades the mayor rides in a howdah on a blown-up elephant,
hit men sip a light Chardonnay opposite their svelte debutantes,
five stories above a distraught mother hurls out an excess child,
illegal aliens are greeted at the dock by agents festooned in red,
a firebrand prophet preaches New Age Thought
offering a lozenge or a placebo of illicit dreams.

And a hooker at 22 is knifed in her love nest,
having witnessed too much of the urban underworld
than is considered seemly for a loquacious lady.

---

1. Paul Zech, "*Fabrikstrasse tags*," Bridgwater, *Twentieth-Century German Verse*, 72.

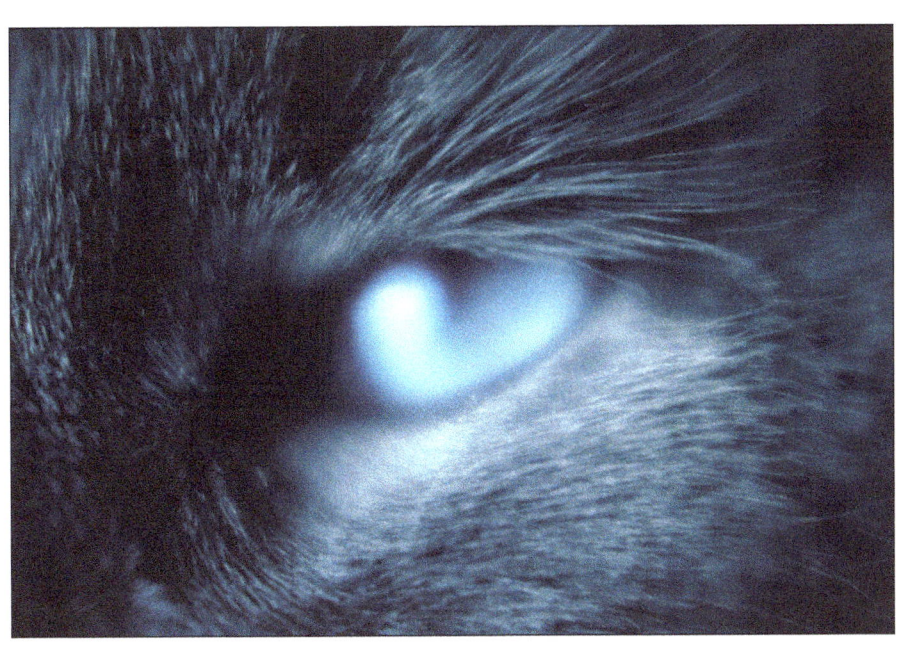

Orwellian Tremors

I have done nothing in secret,
why do you interrogate me behind closed doors
without benefit of witnesses, onlookers?
I believe this to be a house of detention
with no exit but binding and torture.

Already I feel the lock and chains,
cringe at the unendurable silence,
the signed, sleepless confessions,
the nightmarish buttermilk-cracked walls,
the gaunt, screaming inmates.

The *pushmi-pullyu* brainwashing tactics—
I am a crumbling, torn Winston
dreaming of the body of Julia,
too stubborn to submit,
too broken to continue.

Evil lurks in corners unswept by populist anger,
executions are terminal,
disappearances can be propaganda-explained.
Which bootlickers carry out such vile oaths,
where do we breed such rapacious larvae,
and who put cannibals on thrones?

Now Is Madness Come of Age

Now is madness come of age,
the insane loosed from their asylums,
Reason is deposed,
a crowned puppet reigns in his stead,
all is revelry and riotous carnival.

Lunatics parade in papier-mâché,
schizoids like Janus
appear first Dr. Jekyll, then Mr. Hyde,
manics—boisterous—uncontrollably laugh,
transvestites perform in powdered wigs and padded bosoms.

Penitents impale their chests, stomachs, and shoulder blades
with rapiers and long, jagged spikes,
de Sade stretches sobbing, quivering virgins
on racks of anguished, indelicate pain,
around which vicarious voyeurs approve and applaud.

The anal-retentive hoard rusting coppers,
those of unnatural passions resort to custom-fitting,
artificial, complementary organs,
Oedipus sleeps with his Jocasta,
civilization throws off its restraints.

Libertines patrol sidewalks and heated Turkish baths,
Goering attempts palingenesis,
unseemly mediums report pornographic, otherworldly visions,
gods come dressed in crocodile scales, sylvan cat fur,
mothers are in travail over Jupiter's crazed lusts.

Epileptics foam due to demonic, spectral possession,
flute-charmed snakes couple, mysterious stones
are rubbed as love potions or to conjure up
gleaming, all-conquering uncials,
delusion is rampant. Fear, that queen-slut, rules over empires.

II

"The key, the key," cries Moctezuma,
"is this the human Cortés or the living Quetzalcoatl?
My diviner's cup ripples. I'm seasick from staring at the waves.
A huge float bearing a pale, helmeted warrior
will poke out the sun. A night of agonized mirrors begins.

And the extermination of all I thought to be good
by gunpowder bursts and ricocheting cartridges.
Oil lamps of thinly-carved horn run down.
Concheros dancers are lifted high overhead—and dropped.
Nightwatchmen warn of rape, pillage—until they're hoarse and semi-conscious."

First rosé then tawny,
dry before sweet,
light precedes heavy;
as delicately as chardonnay,
wine erases better than bribed Dominican scribblers.

I alone escaped to make clear
that Luna has captured earth's fortress, the Brain:
Chinese boxes contain matryoshka dolls;
knee-deep in the mad slime,
barbarians have come, conquered, and left us diseased.

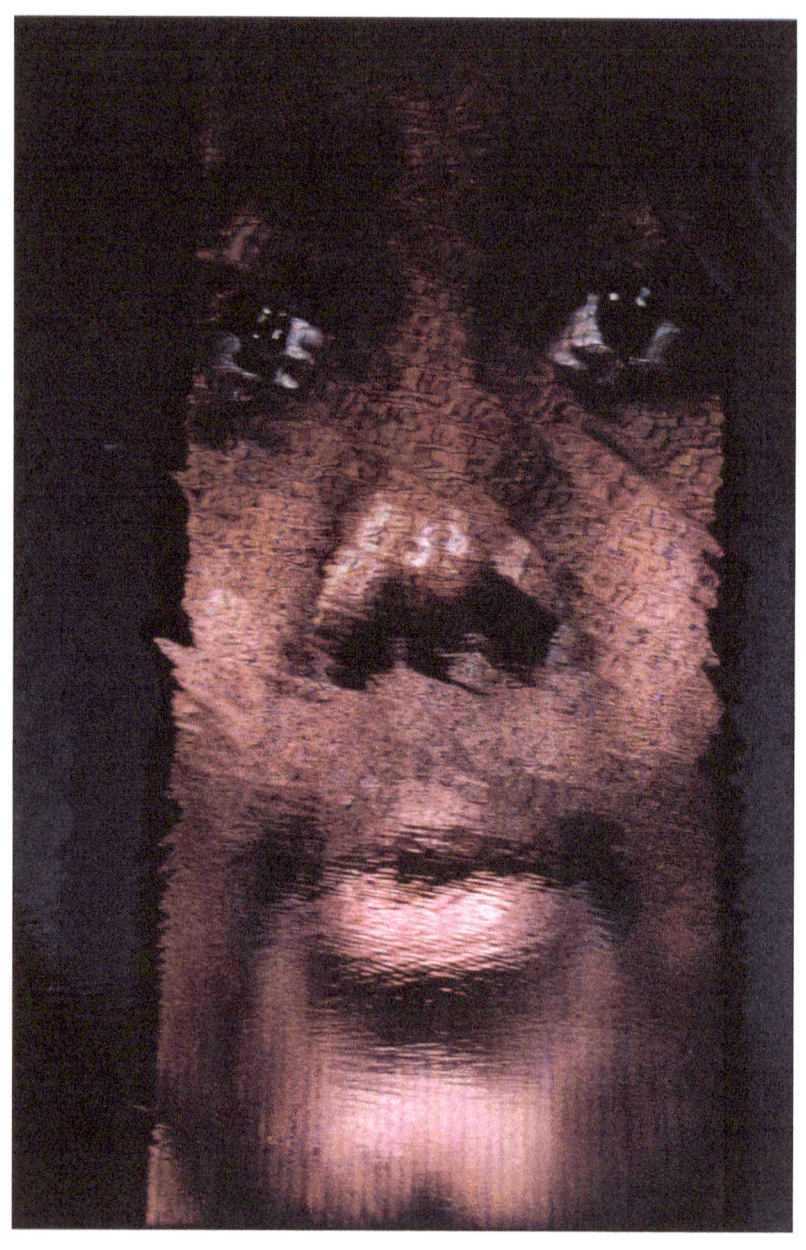

I Shall Go Berserk

I shall go berserk
before those two planets cross,
I shall pipe litany with Mephistopheles
before a fresh communion pass.
Grief will root and tear my heart
before I observe my inner praxinoscope,
counter some unseemly antagonist
—my emotion's powdered fuse.
   Banner headlines, no!
     just scribble out my obituary.

He fiddled, while all about did shout,
paid his rent with the wages from last night's sin.
His unembarrassed broth soiled our city-state:
Medea rage, Hamlet melancholy;
ignotum per ignotius.
Only the Yellow Emperor and Confucius
can distinguish dream from reality,
and aren't they long since dead?

I salivate like an epileptic dog,
see myself in two's (a bifurcate predicament),
talk to my darling parakeet
since mother baked her hemlock pie.
Meow, meow, nods the grandfather clock,
alerting a terrorist incendiary;
Old Yeller wags his tail
to signal Moriarty.

Unplug that bleeping CIA tape,
can I ride on a UFO?
The triffids are swarming
and they're feeding Jimmy Hoffa to them hogs;
the cloud of unknowing is pea green,
I've touched the hollow of God's thigh.

Intercourse is a boomerang
meant to cut off my private parts.
Rasputin, get out from under the sink.
I killed him, mama,
I killed them all!
Can I hatch water moccasins
for the loony house fair?

   Better watch out
or I'll shoot you with a stunkin'-a-ray.
Your honor, I never saw the dead man,
he must be a bloomin' ghost.
Yes, daddy kicked me in the head
and the stars will toss hand grenades.
Judge, your shoes are much too tight and your nose is reindeer red.

Touching Bottom

The acrid air clears,
and the mists and cobwebs
I had entangled myself in
now appear less menacing, overpowering,
like a towering wave which flattens itself against the shore.

I had been wandering in dismal swamp,
then was suddenly transported to lofty peak,
life seemed to me an endless treadmill
until I pulled back abruptly on the brake—
as after a noisy, swords-raised infantry charge,
one counts up casualties and salves the wounded.

But night falls and I grapple with Antaeus angels,
in the morning I'm sore/wounded,
having jousted ferociously with Sir Gawain
till I'm unhorsed and bleeding,
or like a swimmer struggling against a vicious current,
I collapse, gasping and exhausted.

This is lunacy—
to each night undo endless riddles,
agonize over convoluted zigzags,
place a mirror before one's soul;
how much simpler to take a thankless job on the assembly line,
accept wages equal to my competence,
punch a time-clock which circumscribes my duties.

It's so much saner to be bleary-eyed and hung over
than to attempt subliminal Herculean labors—
knocking hard against the profundities of Job—
there the footing is squishy, soft:
who knows if I'll ever touch bottom?

The Light Which Had Been So Keen and Focused

When the cicada breaks its cadence,
the firefly's fuse refuses to ignite,
the grasshopper's titanium wings
turn to tinsel or cellophane,
and the plush, velvety petals of summer
crinkle under an august, bellicose frost.

The light which had been so keen and focused
now lies Inuit-clubbed, gasping, dissipated,
and I'm nocturnally alone with the Alone,
collapsing as a hollow star,
whose veins, unable to discern primary and
secondary perturbations, are overloaded with mercury.

What I had thought would last for ganglia of millennia
now dangles morosely from a quivering thread,
hyper-hope has been reverse-fault buried
under a crustacean bed of dire, irretrievable loss.

Night Turbulence

Nightmares, deep and turbulent,
bloodcurdling as Poe's gothic maelstroms,
puny notions of reality smashed,
unheard of monsters rise from the cavernous muck,
grotesque as Grimm's fairy tales,
the more absurd, the more revelatory.

Friends appear as glutinous blobs of jelly,
ghosts, goblins, vampires slither through partitioned openings,
cityscapes resemble genitalia,
the dead walk about exposing argon-flashing wounds,
lions converse like Cambridge dons,
cottonwoods and toadstools lay bare their spongy souls.
When two kiss, their lips pucker up, seal in wax or bronze,
colors mix and swirl, to fly requires a *Walpurgisnacht* lift-off,
hallucinations are as rampant as the illuminated numerals at Patmos.

Chordates gorge on rock, cacti release their dehydrated needles,
Queen Anne tables lift high their skirts,
internal combustion machines come in opposite sexes, freely reproduce,
dragons are munched by voracious paramecia.
There's a steer with the face of a bat and a vulture with the body of a lynx,
snap your fingers and you'll carouse in some opposite spiraling galaxy,
Boyle can't quite postulate the atom,
and the one you love gleefully toasts to the health of the devil.

Ludicrous Babylon

Jackals prowl, hyenas whine,
the hedgehog roots where prisoners once were tortured,
the palace gardens have been trampled over by invading sheep,
massive walls which once guffawed at the bluster of barbarians
are now crumpled playthings for nomadic children.

Here Marduk and Ishtar once rode high through jubilant streets,
master builders erected spiral or stepped ziggurats,
astrologer-priests scoured the heavens for saturnine portents,
diviners performed hepatoscopy to assuage epidemics,
merchants counted up the inflow, the outflow,
irrigation canals spread out like ebullient webbing,
one heard rumors of far-off marvels: royal incest, warrior elephants,
spices unknown and unsavored by Nimrod's descendants.

What horrid miscalculation led to these sinuous dunes,
where once corridors of bureaucrats had flapped in obeisance,
puppet-governors groveled all along the Fertile Crescent?
Alas, ludicrous Babylon, the dupe of fabulists,
your alleys rollick with tumbleweed,
upstart wildebeest patrol that grandest of boulevards,
philologists garble your most basic conjugation and declension,
while prophets bad-mouth your posturing, preposterous self-aggrandizement.

An Oblong, Inscrutable Alien

I've fallen full fathom five to earth,
an oblong, inscrutable alien
with an improbable message on my blathering lips,
suffocating from a whiff of your ionized atmosphere.

Having traversed googol parsecs, light epochs
through radial arm galaxies, starburst clusters,
I'm so argon-depleted
my memory coils are frozen like a blue icicle.

Did our lab technicians prepare a bleeping capsule
that could be deciphered in alternative biospheres
or has the universal code been rethreaded to fit this peculiar planet's spool?
By which organs do these grotesque creatures interact

and who should be considered the prime or acting species?
Might a comet shatter this blue-green singularity
or some global impact Z-ray,
or has a mutant parasite been introduced with no known anti-toxin?

Have scouts reconnoitered the outer precincts of this ultra-belligerent regime;
is the core's thermostat about to implode?
I'm so jet lag palpitating
that my failsafe corpse is already detonated and glows.

Narcissism

He yearns for sympathetic union
with the one beyond and outside the corporeal self,
reflecting back the inner translucent beauty
of a perfect Platonic sphere,
unbounded by surface mylar,
silver flatland projections;
via strobe-light jagged sequences
he grapples like Antaeus
within a fun house of slanting mirrors.

Ricocheting after each distortion,
more exhausted, less in contact with earth,
as though entrapped
within an autobiographical taleidoscope,
caught in a Kafkaesque landscape crying out
for the real, the genuine Narcissus,
his smooth hands dabble in dreamy water,
ripples destroy the fragile, evanescent whole,
disturbed, undulating half-entities intervene.

If his arms could collapse around
that fetching, sensuous, young fellow,
kiss those silvery, motioning lips,
carry on tête-à-tête with the incommunicable soul,
then might his tears soften,
the fluid boundary be flutteringly agitated,
twin, look-alike spirits reunite,
where the true self spirals in sculpture
more motionless than stone.

Marital Ecology

We pull apart like two species
separated by topography,
I sprout a new runner,
evolve into a religious mutant,
you, you, grow a third eye
and adapt to a sandier environment.

I mimic the flapping beasts
and you crawl away into obscurity,
my brilliant dots and venomous sting
make you burrow further underground,
like two grasses, one saltwater, one fresh,
we mature in quite different terrains.

I filter out impediments to longitudinal growth,
you drink deeply from bayou salts,
once we were climatically similar,
now like an Arctic berg to a Sahara dune,
we live together:
two distinct genera which cannot interbreed.

Our Heap of Merits

Simeon Stylites mounting a cosmic pillar
to extinguish himself for the glory of God,
gurus levitating over the Ganges
due to sacred breathing,
Keswick second-blessings conferences
erupting in glossolalia,
and a Lakota shaman reciting
the coos of the owl and porcupine.

Tibetan mantras and ghoulish sculptures
benumbing subzero pain,
St. Francis and Catherine of Siena
accepting a stigmatic wreath,
Pseudo-Dionysius wedding esoteric doctrine
and neo-Platonism,
Sufis cognizant of the Godhead
in leafy protoplasm.

Piety's perpendicular or
reclining on a bed of spikes,
blasting our preconceptions
with quirks of eccentricity,
overcoming besotted shame and disgrace,
bursting the bonds of respectability.

Save us from guilt-imposed excesses
and erotic self-will,
from grandstanding
and punitive taboos,
from clinging to Nirvana

despite God's admonition,
from emanating vibrations
instead of calloused hands.

This is our heap of merits,
cat's-eye marbles
cracked and scuffed by the flesh—
flawed crystals,
contrived holiness—
we made up the rules.

Approach-Avoid God

Approach-Avoid God,
my squeamish breast,
Sovereign, Redeemer, Bodyguard,
Repressive Father,
Bogeyman with a doomsday book,
Bachelor with one legitimate progeny,
come to the fountain flowing from Immanuel's veins,
ironic laughter,
Deus Absconditus,
+ mercy   – wrath.

me: worm, maggot, lump of sin,
paragon of animals, thinking reed,
contradictory impulses in overdrive,
decently indecent, savagely polite,
the stuff the stars are made of
groveling before metalworkers' gods,
homo ludens, homo faber,
tarnished angel tied to an ass,
weeping for incongruity
+ image of God   – stamp of Adam.

Go into solution like NaCl,
ionic valence or bonded sharing,
assimilation's theoretically impossible,
sapient radical, wholly other catalyst,
affinity for each other, equilibrium achieved,
crystallization can happen
or the current flows—

total coulombs inversely proportional
to square of the distance between charges.

The church particular!
sheep grazing in the meadow,
olive balm, horn to congregate
—one voice, one bishop, one *pantocrator*—
lost, frightened, almost blind,
bleat till wolves or shepherd shows,
trusting, docile creatures will lick
the salt right off your toes,
smelly, wander off effortlessly,
crook to jerk them back in line,
slingshot to scare off predators.

Swarthy archfiend and a fistful
of fellow ruffians, conjuring,
extracting gold from iron pyrite,
heating up the four elements:
combinations, permutations, pseudo-illumination,
are you going to Walpurgis:
Terror of the Night, Lilith,
and cloven-footed Azazel?
sparagmos done in mockery,
transubstantiate the bloody turnip,
evil, the vacuum of God's presence.

Voracious *Thanatos*
eaten up by the Lion of Judah,
a house not built with human hands,
paradoxical joint-ownership,
for better or worse,
the omega point of all ambivalence.

Disembodied You

I sense you in the backlight of ocean-scudding waves,
I feel your presence in still, haunted pools,
when children play jackstraws,
couples flirt beneath a green-tangled canopy,
hikers file singly toward mirage Brigadoon,
you make that loveliest of cameos.

Your smile breaks through the clouds and the foam,
near cascading water, jutting spits and strands,
I run into your clasping hands,
should night close, enwrap, sleep turn to dreams,
you waft in like evening perfume.

Blessed be your cantilever skeleton,
your high pontoon arches, sweeping, suspended strands;
while anchored in the bedrock of my impervious memory,
mists burn off; your steely contours
are more permanent than a poltergeist's;
sway-buckling, you call me across unleapable rifts.

I touch your hummingbird throat,
the hot, tawny recesses of your folded flesh;
muffled laughter I hear,
excited pupils, fingers tremulous and clutching,
angels can't translate the syntax of that pluperfect joy,
though absent, I still discern your disembodied warbling.

The Lingerers at Krakatoa

At the sound of the last trumpet
when time's fluid boundary dissolves
and this wrinkled-up turquoise orb
starts to bobble and shake,
seven marauding angels
will pour out their loathsome vials,
a Newspeak beast and his parrot-toady
will take up the classic demagogue's ruse:
magic, mystery, and regalia.

Two will be absorbed in hoeing, weeding,
and one will be rudely snatched up,
two will be patching, shingling,
and one will poof disappear,
virgins, have you enough oil?
woe to the one who is still nursing,
kneel and beg that the mountains shield your lactating breasts,
pray that your flight not be in winter or during famine,
lest you stumble over frigid or emaciated corpses.

When you view that desolating sacrilege
augured by the vegetarian seer Daniel,
lift up your heads and know that your denouement is near,
for the sun will be blackened and the far side of the moon scorched,
tenebrae blankets all in a morose, suffocating foam,
it is then that you should prop up your weary resolve,
'else destruction will overtake you like those lingerers at Krakatoa.

The House of the Lord

The house of the Lord is in wild disarray,
for its conical steeple has toppled,
its clapper been rudely torn out,
the stained glass Virgin lies splintered
beside soggy, overturned hymnals, soiled prayer books,
the silken altar hangings, too, are crumpled, smeared,
the communion plates and silver candlesticks

tarnished by incessant wind and rain,
the mahogany pulpit is split apart at its seams,
not a few organ stops are missing,
the pews are tilted at crazed angles,
the choir loft is sunk to its gills in muck,
the white, spangled robes have become stained, unangelic,
the altar lies stretched out like the recumbent Christ in a Renaissance Pietà
—all who enter risk decapitation—

the doors which once solemnly closed for adoration of the raised host,
are now creaky, peeling, unadorned,
moss covers the gravestones—attempts at rubbings fail—
merciless time has withered the porcelain Madonna
and twisted the Fourteen Stations of the Cross statuettes and figurines,
only the guest register retains its archaic flavor,
still lying flat, open, and uninviting as a Domesday Book,
if you seek refuge in this temple, better genuflect, then writhe.

A Redemptorist Monk

When I survey the cross
   and the wounds made there by me,
my heart begins to pump
   and my trachea can't breathe,
I sniffle and confess
   a scarlet lack of humility.

When I gaze upon his ankles and his wrists,
   methinks I note vermin
even he cannot forgive,
   a night of indelible ink
splattered across our galaxy,
   a secret wrong or two
his father cannot but damn.

When I bisect his expressionistic head,
   my alarm bell clangs,
I remember an adolescent vice,
   a noble cause I never dared,
a Gospel-thirsty mouth
   I plied with bread and news,
an acquaintance and an ear I never lent.

When I linger about his eyes,
   my rosary beads drop,
my lips start to spread,
   I hurl musty garlands out the door,
weep for worldly pleasures
   too avidly trifled with.

When I analyze his frame,
   'tis but a flatbed truck,
I question my vocation:
   "Am I worthy of his love?"
I take a letter to Father Superior,
   and he gloomily assents.

My Soul

My soul is a pulsing, gleaming lantern
of forged crystal,
endlessly white,
edges beveled,
octahedron, indestructible,
mounted in a setting
of opaque fatty tissue,
whose cleavages show,
impurities discolor;
in this riotous palette
under the curse of amnesia
I lie, a 24-carat flawed
jewel of a boy, whom the devil
wants for a pawn.

Penetrating Light

Light penetrates the darkness
but the darkness refuses to yield,
quanta packets, half-matter, half-vibratory waves
bounce back feeble, uncertain
like wobbly radar blips,
grotesque outlines hover near the ocean floor,
carrying about their own cube of radiant light.

Man is a creature of the day—
not equipped with acute and variable sensors
beyond the revolving eye—
who comprehends via flickers, flashes, wild dilations,
is huddled inside a flimsy scarecrow headdress
deep within a bat-infested cave;
for to fling the unprotected soul
into this nightmarish Megiddo
would engender a second fall.

Just as Aegeus hurled himself off a precipice,
clutch-screaming at nothing
but downturned, smoldering flames,
so the self's boundary is all but extinguished
when darkness usurps the grey, amorphous middle,
and the waters settle into a turgid, sepia calm.
O for a golden draught to be set out in a translucent beaker—
a pure, luminous globe of sheer, soluble enlightenment.

Variations on a Medieval Legend

One does not grow older during time spent at mass
nor in contemplating the three-fold nature of deity,
nor in leading lost sheep to wholesome pasture,
nor in taking a child by a faith-filled hand,
nor in walking through the 14 tear-stained stations of the cross,
nor in looking for the Suffering Servant's reappearing,
nor in chiming bells during compline,
nor in consecrating mundane duties
to Christ's emergent kingdom.

A lark renews itself singing C# arias,
a forest gauzes its burns with fire-resistant cones,
during each and every nature reverie, man sends out fresh and fragrant shoots,
so the infant turns back its parents' clock.

For to age is to stop,
the mind determines the half-life of man,
some wrinkles increase with grey gusto,
on other occasions the heart, like a Japanese cherry blossom,
wavers over a pool of youthful reflections,
a novice peers in,
steals the herb of immortality for a Gilgamesh second . . .

The dates on one's tomb, though chiseled, are insignificant,
precise, yet misleading,
while some dead souls walk about in corporeal caskets
having been stillborn years before,
others never really taste of the coroner's death,
for them ecliptic revolutions are merely timepieces for the unredeemed.

Morituri te Salutamus

Stoke up the fire for Ridley,
Run the sword through Perpetua,
Strangle Tyndale,
Find the largest stones for Stephen,
Crucify Peter upside down.

Let the cannibals munch on Williams,
Aim an arrow at, then pummel, St. Sebastian,
Throw Ignatius to the lions,
Behead Justina,
Hang Bonhoeffer from the gallows.

Gadfly, rebel, or maladjusted freak?
Martyr's libation: the church's gamete,
Demonic rage amplified to a maser's pitch,
Totalitarian roastings, sorcerers stalking,
Intolerance hyped to insanity.

Abu eyes, nerves like a leopard's,
Celtic or Maltese crucifix,
A ribbon of thorns, a bleeding coronet,
Strip eternity of sequential time,
Poach on the Lamb's fledglings.

Better that one should die
Than all civilization admit its guilt,
Confess, confess, thy second birth,
Shroud old Hyde with a Jekyll mask,
Demote Adam or sever his grip.

Murmur "Nearer, My God, to Thee,"
You star of India sapphire,
Glossy or matted impression,
Be a red giant among white dwarfs,
For the crucible means emancipation for the human race.

O Night That Doomed Leviathan

O night that doomed Leviathan
   and pealed our fears to naught,
O Mosaic curtain torn from top to bottom
   by new testament tremors and aftershocks,
O star that nudged Lucifer
   into a nosedive requiem.

O poisoned adder defanged of all
   save his toothless smile,
O deranged dragon
   injected with laughing gas,
O antagonist most comely—
   heel!

O ugly larva,
   metamorphose a monarch lady,
O fleshly centaur,
   step up Darwin's ladder,
O wandering porker in Bunyan mire,
   arise!

A torrent of holy eloquence
   judged Adam, Noah, and Moses' clan,
but at the crossroads of the skull,
   God slashed his tape,
he holds all accountable for how they play their hand—
   some to the royal flush are born,
others take no trick at all,
   —his son is wild!

He flays our debts like the wise magicians at Ephesus
   in one impromptu scourge,
bequeaths us eyes like the belted kingfisher
   to do something beautiful for earth,
he flings our blubbering carcass on his divan
   to rest our libido overload,
his dove perches on a tympanic membrane
   and whispers as to an only child.

He castrates foul autoeroticism
   to lift us to anagogic heights,
and drops us like the bald-headed eagle
   to certify our wings,
tattoos his unequal bride
   by forcing a ring upon her snout,
and plants his honeysuckle gourd
   to wean us from Jonah's mistake.

The Apocalypse

I saw heaven opened
and a tiny angel flutter down
bearing a 600-lb. scroll,
when he spoke the heavens shivered,
his fiery complexion blazed like an unconsumed bush.

The Nile will swallow up Goshen
and cough up red, glowing spume,
igneous mountains march like army ants,
the sun itself will appear to evacuate the vortex,
careen into the inner, lesser planets.

A new and malevolent star bursts forth
dancing its post-mortem jig,
the kings of the east will unleash lightning warfare in the Valley of Josaphat,
locusts attack in phalanx rotation,
a false prophet and ten-horned beast join hands with a centuries-old dragon.

Two witnesses will jump up from their caskets
and call for El Cid to intervene,
what of that great whore, Babylon,
who incubates every pimp, every john?
the Devil himself conjuring up pseudo-incarnation.

An opaque veil will encrust their hearts,
wax seals for times and half a time,
illuminated digits appear in cipher code
on the foreheads of appointed victims,
while squadrons of fallen angels encircle Gog and Magog.

An intergalactic satellite will lock onto earth's cooling orbit,
a garden be replenished from hybrid, uncontaminated stock,
gold blossom in the calyx of the black-eyed Susan,
evil simmer nearly vanquished
in a pond radiating sulfurous fumes.

Hallelujah choruses will blanket the minimalist earth,
an invisible purifying stream flows as if from a catalytic converter,
Michael himself leading evensong,
then I saw the Pierced One cauterized on the left side of his throne.

If I Could But Touch Peace . . .

If I could but touch peace
dripping down in harmonious strings
from a beeswax mold,
reside in a rustic, hand-hewn log cabin
seated before a roaring flame,
if I could put my hands out
and still my turbulent conscience,
tell no more outright lies,
abandon mad pursuit of pleasure and gain,
greet my neighbor with unfeigned smile,
if I could hold a nugget of truth,
assay, measure, and stabilize its proportions,
enrich all with a honeyed residue,
then couch it in exalted phrase,
that would be enough—
but whether I do what's truly virtuous
or follow some less sympathetic lark
is the Sphinx-like enigma I cannot unravel.

The Paschal Candle

When shadows congregate and lengthen,
doomsayers stump the soapbox circuit,
thunderclaps reverberate like battlefield artillery shells,
I light my Paschal candle
to cloak a hazel viper's stare.

After three days of lamentation, *Tenebrae*, Gloria Patri forgot,
a wooden Jesus wheeled about on a wooden ass,
an emerging sarcophagus is glorified, carrying the red banner of resurrection,
his sacred purple monogram: *A* and *O*,
misericords redeemed, *schola cantorum*.

All baptized must drink from this descended columbine,
a virgin egg hatching of its own accord,
scissored, whipped, hammered, nailed,
Christ rides on a scarlet horse through a grove
of myrtle, followed by row after row of martyrs' stallions.

A Baaing Lamb

The living bird shall be set free
when the leper is certifiably clean,
we'll shoot off rockets and tambourine flares
if the demoniac sits as calmly as you or I,
the deaf sense wave-vibrations, the blind are bewitched by colors,
the poor recover spiritual riches,
and no one takes offense
at the mangled, beaten Messiah.

A lost coin, a sheep who wanders off,
a husk-eating prodigal son or daughter—
may they not be compared to the pearl of inestimable price?
the lilies of the field, the birds of the air,
bow down before his providential hand,
while mankind is the lone dissenter,
to what shall I liken the kingdom of light,
a bubbling fountain of perpetual youth?

Angels descend in invigorating hailstorms,
horns sprout up from a monstrous ganglion head,
a women in travail laments, stars fall into flaming rivers,
Michael rides a dappled colt to do battle with a titanic dragon,
trumpets blare, a third of the earth staggers,
these three beasts arise: a winged lion, a leopard, a bear,
evil is subdued by a meek, baaing lamb
who stands triumphant on a gilded Flemish Assize throne.

How Shall the Dead Arise?

How shall the dead arise—
in velvet loops and powdered wigs?
skeleton-stripped?
blushing but elegant?
robust June or wintry deciduous?
one happy birthday or of a double horoscope?

Adam's sperm peopled a universe,
Quousque, Domine?
limbo yawns like a fairway trap
before our Jubilee,
'midst a rotunda of well-wishers
we lie cardiac still,
they slap 12 spokes to a rim
and call it a funereal wheel.

Go forth a recombinant 21st-century man
drilled through by Namtar's metallic grin,
freeze-dried parchment, organs transplanted,
test tube regurgitate,
the doors of the temple are opened
and the stone rolled away.

Night is with child and day has already conceived,
the dark barrow, a neon firstfruits marquee,
Plotinus' snake glides into its hole,
Fan Li embarks in his boat with Xi Shi, then disappears,
in the mirrored pool the Ideal and Real meet,
my dead bones rattle like an old tin roof,
heron reborn.

Revelation 7:9–10

From out of the slime,
from the frozen wastes
teeming with life,
from 25th-century urbanscapes
peopled by recombinant silicon:
the City Foursquare set in the Gospel Tabernacle.

How shall they praise him
that have no tongue?
How shall they view the Lamb
without any retina?
Biped, crustacean, millipede—
marvels enough to make
discrimination by skin passé.

The scale of being multiplied
in Pythagorean tetrads—
paean to cosmic diversity.
Uniform symmetry
is the devil's keenest tool
to mass-produce conformists
worthy of a despot.

Will they kneel on their mats five
times a day like a Musulman?
Will their incorruptible suits
grow a pineal gland?

Can they shout Hallelujah
from head to ankle—
the Holy Ghost himself banging the piano?

Springy antenna, club fists, marsupial placenta,
invisible, divisible, basically imaginary,
isotope twins, look-a-like antipodes, fully reversible organs,
asexual reproduction, fission, mitosis,
carnivorous, herbivore, cannibal-aholics,
ESP, telepathy, astral projection.

Gorgon heads, effluence of desiccation.
Yet God's portrait is in the alcoves of every soul, *sic passim*.
Turn up the volume, *te Deum laudamus*.

To What Shall I Compare the Kingdom of Heaven?

The Kingdom of Heaven is like a staircase
   that spirals up the Cosmic Tree.
The Kingdom of Heaven is like a candle,
   which once lit, is never puffed out.
The Kingdom of Heaven is like three polygons
   which converge into a prism.
The Kingdom of Heaven is like a pearl button
   closing up our culpability.
The Kingdom of Heaven is like a daffodil
   bearing the incense of reborn spring.
The Kingdom of Heaven is like a groom and bride
   whose wedding and funeral coincide.
The Kingdom of Heaven is like a mystic book
   imparting prevenient grace to all who read.
The Kingdom of Heaven is like a tear
   overflowing into perpetual oblivion.

Come, Holy Spirit

Come, Holy Spirit,
anoint my lips with fire,
I am injured and sore oppressed
from my own boomerang desires,
every thought is fraught with duplicity,
every act tainted by concupiscence.

Oh, who can deliver me from this seething vat,
firmly plant my feet on unshakeable ground?
while all about are scoffers, tempters,
demons intent on pulling me into the swirling abyss,
they whisper cheery, soothing melodies,
rhythmic tempos which cloak a final requiem.

Sometimes I believe I can obtain
laurels without an all-out ordeal,
pasture in green arbors and herb-scented meadows,
and not have my foundations pulled apart,
nor dice spit out two venomous eyes,
nor multitudes groan under iron decrees.

I love the exuberant sun, the light-dancing streams,
the luscious, ripe, candied fruit,
but I've an appointment beyond the grave
to which the celestial clock compels me to run,
where, o where, are childhood gurglings, fleshly embraces
in that intimate, yet incorporeal, sphere?

There all longings coalesce into one excited ball,
questions stoke gentle illumination,
zeal, indignation, vehemence
melt into love's foaming plenitude,
self-seeking disruptive mechanisms
are not so much as conceived.

A Rabelaisian Yuletide

Make we mirth
for Christ's live birth
and sing we Yule until Candlemas.

Reptiles bite and grasp and gnaw,
amebae tear paramecia apart,
carnivores lick their salivating chops,
for all of life is one splendiferous morsel,
though the distended gullet is never satiated,
space curdles, time crinkles up,
Balaam's ass cavorts and bellows,
and we're off to Bethlehem, tra la!

Dendrites are hollowed out part-manger, part-crucifix,
the womb coalesces into one exuberant howl
and out jumps that preternatural prankster, the almos' human boy,
jangling his cap and bells,
oh, thanks be to the Prime Mover
that the Devil can't lift a hangnail
against this bipartite griffin
snoring in a Franciscan crèche.

Matins we intone and evensong we chant
since the Absolute has condescended to enflesh himself as a lowly mammal,
but the Creator's been rebuffed by all he's animated,
the Potter discarded by his meanest pots,
the Sovereign overthrown and trampled upon by disloyal subjects,
thus justice has fled down a sinkhole
where it shivers in old Fahrenheit,
awaiting typological fulfillment.

II

I say, sir, you are a magnificent worm,
though you grovel quite insincerely,
it does a body good to weep and gnash
on account of previously unbuttoned shenanigans,
aren't you that slithering rodent
who once bat-flitted through Gotham's cavernous shadows?
I plotted a great circle route
and, of course, it penetrated my mistress' buttocks.

Topers toast and re-toast heady foam,
has a wild child ever conversed fluently in rhyme
without coaching from the king's own lexicographer,
reciting poetic cupcakes, palindrome wreaths,
curlicue trinkets, twanging toys,
then gone wassailing in the mummer's fashion?
the crowds are primed for pyrotechnic extravaganza,
the hurdy-gurdy monkey gambols about on stilts.

Waiter, fill up this blasted tankard,
since the dead lie listless in parsimonious rows
savoring their scooped-out anonymity,
while rutile marbles ricochet in rotting craniums,
doesn't Athens flow into St. Petersburg, the Euphrates inundate Jerusalem,
and every bald-faced lie I've told is existentially valid in some anti-world?
Word without contour, Word without shape,
like some newborn Hottentot's fricative spasms.

III

Miracles ride into town disguised as symbiotic twins,
aren't Jachin and Boaz allotropes,
cartwheeling, somersaulting startsy

shimmering beneath their rhomboid nimbuses?
are those angelic intruders still detaining father Abraham?
is it possible that 5 loaves and 2 small fish
could sustain all 144,000 sealed from the tribes of Jacob?

The pillars of Asherah have been hacked down and pulverized,
the chariots of the sun melted into filigreed bracelets and rings,
the vessels and utensils dedicated to Baal purified,
and this unwieldy crew of silversmiths,
mercenary priests, and pseudo-prophets
are near to being roasted upon an open pyre,
their zoomorphic talismans and amulets
smolder on the half-converted chaparral.

So, heave off your enervated idols,
dangling puppets, and ornamental marionettes
lisping in the Pinocchio fashion,
carried about by lackeys on alabaster pallets
—all oracles are mere subterfuges—
hysteria is regarded as a symptom of deluded possession,
riddles themselves are deliberately embroiled in ambiguity,
Nostradamus himself being the chief perpetrator.

IV

Who will ascend the heights to bring Christ down,
shall Elijah shoot up in his prop jet chariot,
or who will descend into Tartarus to bring up Christ's radiant corpse,
shall rebellious, earth-swallowed Korah?
God sucks on Virgin's dugs,
then soils his undies.

If the eye is scratched, the whole body swells
into a white-out eclipse or some murky penumbra,

like Diogenes I carry a heat-seeking lantern
which hones in on those who are lowly and unpretentious,
for some duplicitous pedlar in divinity
has noxiously carted away our starry aspirations.
Still, the Emmaus Road is crackling with serendipitous incursions,
more real than any manufactured at Lourdes or Pentecostal pep rallies.

Iacta Alea Esto

What ever happened to Matthias—
odd man out, 13th apostle, God's second string?
Did he ignominiously receive the scarlet A?
lie to the Holy Ghost, see God's averted face?
hear a call to the land of the *anthropophagi*, end up in another's digestive tract?

Was it he who blessed the holy mother with a virginal fruit fly?
lost the crown of thorns, synthesized a relic?
confused Jesus and Mithra, was baptized in a *taurobolium*?
harangued the multitude as the first Docetic-Gnostic-Manichee?

After a few nips, advocated uncircumcising the Ebionites,
christened his ass "Lord Balaam," caught delirium tremens,
sprouted wings in a beatific vision, became earth's second satellite,
climbed the pillars of the temple, fasted for 231 days,
performed no miracles, joined up with Simon Magus?

Led the first crusade to Mt. Gerizim, hung Samaritans on Herod's door,
evangelized Caesar's household, was the whipping boy for Nero's violin,
composed Q, then circulated it in south Galatia,
committed fornication—shacked up with Mary Magdalene,
organized a protest march to Antonia, was crucified a Zealot?

Aspired to the bishopric, but didn't have the pull,
won for himself enviable deeds, but couldn't afford a chronicler,
or simply lapsed into oblivion like we his successors do?

Numeral Occult

1,461 years since last the Phoenix came,
a millennium in which Jesus reigns,
7 x 7 x 70 since Abram left Ur
and 33 to the third power since Pythagoras' last reverie,

watch 44 do a handspring,
666 brand itself on your forehead,
irrational numbers stump the philosophers
and logarithms roll around in cylinders,

ecstatic equations ricocheting in Euclid's head,
Archimedes pouring them into Syracuse's defenses,
Newton calculating an earthquake-proof floor,
Einstein registering at 9.1 on Richter's scale,

elliptical Kepler or epicyclical Ptolemy,
a spiraling nautilus whole,
what of the magnitude of the Milky Way,
Hubble's expanding universe, the possibility of superlunary life?

collapse your hands around any whole number
and it disintegrates and decimals revert to powder,
bipartite or triune hominid:
negative weight equivalent to 0,

separate the real from the imaginary,
lest a chimera gum up your cipher,
put right angles opposite obtuse
so that vectors cross-triangulate,

hew fractions to their lowest common denominator,
pull out your transposition wheel or Polybius square,
God himself is split in three,
the square root of 9 multiplied a thousandfold.

Soul Vibes

Prop up your drooping hands,
strengthen those weak and feeble knees,
gesticulate with Alleluia fingers,
shout Salvation from chin to toe,
swaying to the rhythms of a brass-string band—
accompanied by a loud chorus of foot-stomping Amens.

Wiggle your backbone with a mighty unction,
harmonize like the eight-part a capella of angelic choirs,
thank you, thank you, thank you, Jesus
in excited *Maranatha* modes,
intercede with cymbals, rattles, and bells,
jingle-jangling praise emanates from the inheavings of the soul,
recite *Kyrie eleison* in a meditative trance,
echoing the *Bath Kol*'s sighings and murmurings,
open wide your being for an infusion of primum mobile love.

Tear out that rigid, stony heart,
replace it with one that zings,
if there's anything God detests,
it's a smug and solemn statuette.
Rise up and gyrate like an inebriated dervish,
jump and bound, skip and leap,
link hands in a dancing Shaker circle,
for there's a crackling dynamo known as YHWH,
who electrifies any vertebrate left standing still.

Yurodivy: The Holy Fool

He leaps and frolics,
performs somersaults, cartwheels, then stands on his head—
with clanging gongs and jingling tambourines,
he issues heave-ho harangues,
then ricochets off the ceiling,
howls and giggles, weeps profusely,
glides across the countertop topsy-turvy.

A lunatic trapeze artist,
he assumes a non-stop repertoire of outlandish shapes,
like a master hypnotist or Hindu fakir,
he transfixes reptilian hisses and gazes,
or like a meteoric Cicero
rows up and down the Bay of Profundities,
bludgeoning the sensual, tweaking the complacent,
revivifying ossified sinners.

Emanations glow from his innermost cells,
from his brow sweat drops red as compassion,
multitudes seek relief via his therapeutic fingers,
in his presence profane objects are mystically transfigured,
his wonder-working mantle and prophetic spirit
are bequeathed to onlookers like relics,
even his dung appears limpid and holy.

That Amethyst Chariot

Let me board that amethyst chariot
which courses through land and air,
sink down into its sheltering upholstery
as a motherless, blubbering child
carried off past a flotilla of metallic ribbons
toward a supersaturate Magellanic cloud,
led on as Arjuna into battle
past the Strong Man and the Generalissimo,
as though the entire mélange had been preordained.

Angelic arias arise in counterpoint, syncopation,
bogus nimbuses recede,
winged cherubim and seraphim descend,
while I converse ignitedly with Moses and Elijah;
from my suspended Socratic bulrush basket,
wheels spin within the sprockets of interlocking wheels,
and I'm bewildered by that twinkle in God's eye,
keen to arrive, panting, much athirst
at the epicenter where I began so long ago.

When the Soul Quits the Earthly Body

When the soul quits the earthly body,
there'll be no more of Innisfree,
tears interwoven into the fabric,
the dull yellow of our solar system
is jettisoned away,
Technicolor, 3-D jottings
transfixed into gratitude,
the static of clashing auras vaporized,
blinders slipping off our retinas
and pores immersed in tranquility,
there you'll find your El Dorado,
where the Pishon and Gihon have their springs,
the multi-ethnic Jesus will gather his intergalactic flock,
and this gray world will be as a foghorn in the night.

On Eternity's Shore Looking Back

Time has stopped making quantitative distinctions,
a second ticks off nonchalantly as a 24-hour axial revolution,
epochs, aeons, megacycles
are as nothing compared to eternity's scale,
all these infinite expanses can be contained within a protozoa's vacuole,
life's significance grows dull as a cardboard razor,
the dialogues of Plato, Aristotle's categories, Kant's imperatives
—the twaddle of unformed embryos—
physical space itself is a matter of non-falsifiable conjecture,
atoms are as deceptive as light,
perceiving and not-perceiving as nonsensical as a Zen koan,
I, a fluid, collective pronoun,
once memories, relationships, objects appeared tangible,
now the fully synthesized data takes on a grander, more unified schematic,
I used to picture Christ as a stationary, changeless pyramid,
but in actuality the Godhead oscillates, transcending all envelopes of reason.

II Corinthians 3

The splendor of Moses' face
is being brushed into
more neutral tones,
his temporal veil is slowly lifted
and we are transformed
by runic, paternoster mirrors,
the old sinful self expires daily,
the passions, once aroused, flaunted,
are strangled by painful self-asphyxiation.

Previously bound *douloi*, now gleeful servants,
where the Spirit of the Lord is,
there liberty reigns,
as muted trumpeter swans
we celebrate our life in death,
step precipitously down from the smoking, belching heights,
all covered with ashes and a fiery, supernatural glow.

What we behold, we become,
Christ's embryo is formed inside our ovaries
destroying unregenerate cancerous cells,
the container cannot contain the contained
like the Minotaur loosed from a Knossos labyrinth,
the dead pass from one magnitude of brightness to one unexcelled,
shadow puppets who, at last, see the sun face-to-face.

Listing of Photographs

1. Shadow of hand and circle of light [Heaven, A Fantasy with Explanatory Digressions]
2. Woman on dirt road with storm clouds [A Day Like No Other]
3. Old photo of soldier in a frame [Deceitful Time]
4. Woman standing in steam in front of gate [All Is Smoke]
5. Pebbles on beach near water [Time Is . . .]
6. Looking through multi-colored glass on veranda, Sarasota Springs [The Whining Mandolin]
7. Reflections of shadows of passersby on sidewalk [The Dance of Death]
8. Male manikin head and torso lying beside legs [Delusion]
9. Close-up of woman's head on bed [A Night of Peacock Eyes]
10. Anguished girl holding hands as if in prayer [The Reluctant Left Hand of God]
11. Colored umbrellas all in a row ["There Was Silence . . ."]
12. Men reading at Penn Station, New York [The Meaning Flowed On]
13. Sunset along Connecticut River, red filter [On a June Evening]
14. Drunk lying near wall painting [*Nichts als Mauern*"]
15. Close-up of cat's eye [Orwellian Tremors]
16. Colorful wigs in shop window, New Orleans [Now is Madness Come of Age]

17. Reflection of face, Millennium Park, Chicago [I Shall Go Berserk]
18. Wavy reflections in water, Metropolitan Museum of Art [Touching Bottom]
19. Sunlight on milkweeds near Lancaster, NH [The Light Which Had Been So Keen and Focused]
20. Woman standing in glittering water, blue filter [Night Turbulence]
21. Ruins of Persepolis in Iran [Ludicrous Babylon]
22. Woman with exaggerated legs in mirror [An Oblong, Inscrutable Alien]
23. Girls near distorting mirrors, Navy Pier, Chicago [Narcissism]
24. Silhouettes of man, woman and child at beach [Marital Ecology]
25. Sufi dervish in Iran [Our Heap of Merits]
26. Stained glass showing Father holding crucified Son [Approach-Avoid God]
27. Fall leaf in rippling water [Disembodied You]
28. Shoe shine of woman at New Orleans bar [The Lingerers at Krakatoa]
29. Adobe church and cemetery at Taos, NM [The House of the Lord]
30. Crucifix, Mission San Luis Obispo de Tolosa, CA [A Redemptorist Monk]
31. Frowning boy with lollipop [My Soul]
32. Sun peeping behind barren trees [Penetrating Light]
33. Priest at chapel in St. John the Divine Cathedral [Variations on a Medieval Legend]
34. Tombstones at New Orleans cemetery [*Morituri te Salutamus*]
35. Evangelist in Manhattan [O Night that Doomed Leviathan]
36. Bronze Jesus with holes in hands, Church of St. John the Baptist in Manhattan [The Apocalypse]
37. Fall fishing, Connecticut River, Turner Falls, MA [If I Could But Touch Peace . . .]
38. Candle flame [The Paschal Candle]
39. Sheep grazing in Utah [A Baaing Lamb]

40. Tombstone at Christ Church, Frederica, GA [How Shall the Dead Arise?]
41. Marionettes in store window [Revelation 7:9–10]
42. Woman reading among trees in fog [To What Shall I Compare the Kingdom of Heaven?]
43. Pigeon flying above fountain [Come, Holy Spirit]
44. Adoration of the Christ Child stained glass, Faith Chapel, Jekyll Island, GA [A Rabelaisian Yuletide]
45. Man walking on sidewalk beside shadow [*Iacta Alea Esto*]
46. Front view of no. 2 train engine [Numeral Occult]
47. Woman on spinning merry-go-round [Soul Vibes]
48. Window washer at Flatiron Building [*Yurodivy*: The Holy Fool]
49. Chapel window, Epworth-by-Sea, St. Simons Island, GA [That Amethyst Chariot]
50. Island on reservoir, Tarrytown, NY [When the Soul Quits the Earthly Body]
51. Cross in Chapel of the Transfiguration at Grand Tetons [On Eternity's Shore Looking Back]
52. Man sunning himself with reflector in Manhattan [II Corinthians 3]

Works Cited

Aune, David. *Revelation 17-22: Word Biblical Commentary*. Nashville: Thomas Nelson, 1998.
Augustine. *The City of God*. Translated by Henry Bettenson. New York: Penguin, 1984.
———. *City of God (Abridged)*. Translated by Gerald G. Walsh, et al., edited by Vernon J. Bourke. New York: Image, 1958.
———. *The Retractions*. Translated by Sister Mary Inez Bogan. Washington, DC: Catholic University Press of America, 1968.
Bavinck, Herman. *Reformed Dogmatics, Volume 4: Holy Spirit, Church, and New Creation*. Translated by John Vriend, edited by John Bolt. Grand Rapids: Baker, 2008.
Baxter, Jason M. *An Introduction to Christian Mysticism: Recovering the Wildness of the Spiritual Life*. Grand Rapids: Baker, 2021.
Baxter, Richard. *The Saints' Everlasting Rest*. Monroe, IL: Pantianos, 2021.
Beal, Timothy. *The Book of Revelation: A Biography*. Princeton, NJ: Princeton University Press, 2018.
Beale, G.K. *Revelation: A Shorter Commentary*. Grand Rapids: Eerdmans, 2015.
Boersma, Hans. *Seeing God: The Beatific Vision in Christian Tradition*. Grand Rapids: Eerdmans, 2018.
Bourke, Vernon J., ed. *The Pocket Aquinas*. New York: Washington Square, 1964.
Bridgwater, Patrick, ed. *Twentieth-Century German Verse*. Baltimore: Penguin, 1963
Bunyan, John. *The Pilgrim's Progress*. Edited by Roger Sharrock. London: Penguin, 1987.
Burk, John N. "Symphony in D Minor, No. 9." In *The Analytical Concert Guide*, edited by Louis Biancolli, 68. Garden City, NY: Doubleday, 1951.
Catholic Church. *Catechism of the Catholic Church*. San Francisco: Ignatius, 1994.
St. Cyprian of Carthage. *The Letters, Volume III:55-66*. Translated by G.W. Clarke. Mahwah, NJ: Newman Press, 1986.
Danielou, Jean, ed. *From Glory to Glory: Texts from Gregory of Nyssa's Mystical Writings*. Translated by Herbert Musurillo. Crestwood, NY: St. Vladimir's Seminary Press, 1979.
Dante Alighieri. *The Divine Comedy: Paradiso*. Translated by Charles S. Singleton. Princeton, NJ: Princeton University Press, 1982.

Eusebius of Caesarea. *The History of the Church: A New Translation*. Translated by Jeremy M. Schott. Oakland, CA: University of California Press, 2019.

Gallagher, Joseph. *To Hell and Back with Dante: A Modern Reader's Guide to The Divine Comedy*. Liguori, MO: Triumph, 1996.

Gregg, Rev. David. *The Heaven-Life Or Stimulus For Two Worlds*. New York: Fleming H. Revell, 1895.

Saint Gregory of Nyssa. *Ascetical Works*. Washington, DC: Catholic University Press of America, 1967.

———. *On the Soul and the Resurrection*. Crestwood, NY: SVS Press, 1993.

Hackforth, R., trans. "Phaedrus." In *The Collected Dialogues of Plato, Including the Letters*, edited by Edith Hamilton and Huntington Cairns. Princeton, NJ: Princeton University Press, 1989.

Harris, C. "State of the Dead (Christian)." In *Encyclopedia of Religion and Ethics, Volume XI*, edited by James Hastings, 834. Edinburgh: T&T Clark, 1920.

Heilbroner, Robert L. *The Worldly Philosophers: The Lives and Ideas of the Great Economic Thinkers, Fourth Edition*. New York: Simon & Schuster, 1972.

Hildegard of Bingen. *The Book of the Rewards of Life*. Translated by Bruce W. Hozeski. New York: Oxford University Press, 1997.

Hind, Rebecca. *The Faces of God: 1000 Images in Art*. London: Carlton Books, 2012.

Jeffery, Arthur, ed. *Islam: Muhammad and His Religion*. Indianapolis: Bobbs-Merrill, 1958.

Johnson, Samuel. *Rasselas, Poems, and Selected Prose, Third Edition*. Edited by Bertrand H. Bronson. San Francisco: Rinehart, 1971.

Kelly, J.N.D. *Early Christian Doctrines*. New York: Harper & Row, 1960.

Kirk, K.E. *The Vision of God: The Christian Doctrine of the Summum Bonum*. New York: Harper & Row, 1996.

Kovacs, Judith and Christopher Rowland. *Revelation: Blackwell Bible Commentaries*. Malden, MA: Blackwell, 2004.

Kramer, Ross S., ed. *Maenads, Martyrs, Matrons, Monastics: A Sourcebook on Women's Religions in the Greco-Roman World*. Philadelphia: Fortress, 1988.

Leibniz. *Philosophical Writings*. London: J.M. Dent & Sons, 1977.

Lewis. C.S. *The Great Divorce*. New York: HarperCollins, 2001.

———. *The Last Battle*. New York: Macmillan, 1976.

———. *The Problem of Pain*. New York: Macmillan, 1956.

———. *The Weight of Glory and Other Addresses*. Grand Rapids: Eerdmans, 1977.

Lucian. *Selected Satires of Lucian*. Translated by Lionel Casson. New York: Norton, 1968.

Mawson, C.O. Sylvester. *Dictionary of Foreign Terms, Second Edition*. Revised and updated by Charles Berlitz. New York: Barnes & Noble, 1979.

McDannell, Colleen and Bernhard Lang. *Heaven: A History*. New York: Random House, 1990.

McGrath, Alister. *A Brief History of Heaven*. Malden, MA: Blackwell, 2003.

Oden, Thomas C. *Life in the Spirit: Systematic Theology, Volume 3*. New York: Harper SanFrancisco, 1992.

O'Hear, Natasha and Anthony O'Hear. *Picturing the Apocalypse: The Book of Revelation in the Arts Over Two Millennia*. Oxford: Oxford University Press, 2017.

Origen. *On First Principles*. Translated by G.W. Butterworth. Notre Dame, IN: Ave Maria, 2013.

Parrinder, Geoffrey. *Dictionary of Religious and Spiritual Quotations*. New York: Simon & Schuster, 1989.
Patai, Raphael. *The Messiah Texts*. New York: Avon, 1979.
Pseudo-Dionysius. *The Complete Works*. Translated by Colm Luibheid. Mahwah, NJ: Paulist, 1987.
Puppi, Lionello. *El Greco*. New York: Grosset & Dunlap, 1967.
Richardson, E.P. *A Short History of Painting in America: The Story of 450 Years*. New York: Crowell, 1963.
Russell, Jeffrey Burton. *A History of Heaven: The Singing Silence*. Princeton, NJ: Princeton University Press, 1997.
Ruusbroec, John. *The Spiritual Espousals and Other Works*. Translated by James A. Wiseman. Mahwah: NJ: Paulist, 1965.
Sernett, Milton, C., ed. *Afro-American Religious History: A Documentary Witness*. Durham, NC: Duke University Press, 1988.
Singer, Isaac Bashevis. *Love and Exile: An Autobiographical Trilogy*. New York: Farrar Straus Giroux, 1984.
Speiser, E.A., trans. "The Epic of Gilgamesh." In *The Ancient Near East: An Anthology of Texts and Pictures*, edited by James B. Pritchard, 40. Princeton, NJ: Princeton University Press, 2011.
Stewart, Bryan A. & Michael A. Thomas, trans. and eds. *John: Interpreted by Early Christian and Medieval Commentators*. Grand Rapids: Eerdmans, 2018.
Trenckner, V., ed. "Milindapanha." In *Sources of Indian Tradition, Volume One: From the Beginning to 1800, Second Edition*, edited and revised by Ainslie T. Embree. New York: Columbia University Press, 1998.
Trigg, John Wilson. *Origen: The Bible and Philosophy in the Third-century Church*. Atlanta: John Knox, 1983.
Valla, Lorenzo. *On Pleasure: De Voluptate*. Translated by A. Kent Hieatt and Maristella Lorch. New York: Abaris, 1977.
Vaus, Will. *Mere Theology: A Guide to the Thought of C.S. Lewis*. Downers Grove, IL: InterVarsity, 2004.
Virgil. *The Aeneid*. Translated by W. Jackson Knight. Baltimore: Penguin, 1963.
Watson, Thomas. *The Beatitudes*. Monroe, IL: Independently published, 2021.
Watts, Isaac. *Works, Published by Himself, Volume 2*. Charleston, SC: Nabu Press, 2012.
Zaleski, Carol. "When I Get to Heaven." *Christian Century* (5 April 2003).
Zaleski, Carol and Philip Zaleski, eds. *The Book of Heaven: An Anthology of Writings from Ancient to Modern Times*. New York: Oxford University Press, 2000.

www.ingramcontent.com/pod-product-compliance
Lightning Source LLC
Chambersburg PA
CBHW042128160426
43198CB00021B/2944